Only One
How to be a *Bad Ass* Boss in Corporate America

Only One
How to be a *Bad Ass* Boss in Corporate America

Monica M. Brown

NEW Reads Publications | Jacksonville

I dedicate this book to my parents, Louis and Gloria Brown, and my daughters, Lakeva Brown and Madison Mathis. Special dedication to my heavenly angels Albertha P. Williams and Christina James. This book is for you!

Contents

Introduction   i

1. The Journey Begins   2
2. Transformation to Determination   10
3. The Dynamics of You   20
4. You are Aggressive! (And Not in a Good Way)   34
5. Your Network is Your Next Opportunity   43
6. Characteristics of a *Bad Ass* Executive   55
7. Hire One, Get One Free   69
8. Know Your Worth   79
9. Everything You Do Matters   89
10. They Tried It!   99
11. The Next Level   113
12. The Room Scan   119

Perspectives   130
Notes from the Next Generation   138
Acknowledgements   144
Bibliography   148

Introduction

In recent years, I've had the amazing privilege of speaking on numerous panel discussions and participating in conferences to talk about my experience being a Black female executive in corporate America. For some reason, be it odd or justified, other women seeking to elevate their careers are intrigued by the fact that I was able to break the glass ceiling. Possibly because I am a rare sight among those you normally see in high level corporate positions. Even though it's sad the glass ceiling still exists, and for now it seems I am the exception when it comes to the various positions I've held across various Fortune 500 companies, I do not have to be the rule.

I believe every woman of color and every person of color understands that there are differences in how we are viewed, treated, and revered in corporate settings. An unspoken understanding often clearly demonstrates the rules may be slightly different for us than they are for everybody else. Yet each day, we show up to work, dressed like everyone else so we fit in. We adjust our dialect to diminish or completely erase our home-grown accents so as not to be misconstrued as being ignorant or less educated because of where we come from. Assimilating, conforming, code-switching and normalizing who we are to more easily gain the support of those who seemingly hold the key to our success is just part of what it takes to move up the corporate ladder.

Imagine the need to do this twice! Not only lightly erasing traces of your heritage, but also trying to overcompensate for your gender in a male-dominant environment. Well, it's something I've done on numerous occasions. Too many to count and more than I would care to admit. Watching the mannerisms and digesting the responses of others in reaction to me, a Black Woman, so that I can figure out how to use their same references in future conversations.

For example, I have been called "aggressive" in a negative tone, while my male counterparts have been praised as "assertive" for actions and reactions identical to my own. I have been challenged in meetings by my own male direct reports and peers because they couldn't handle the banter from a minority woman who knew just as much, if not more than them in that moment. Despite the blatant disrespect, I quickly learned that being a Black woman in corporate America comes with hurdles and challenges, moments of disbelief and shock, and even moments of "lemme take off my earrings and show you what's really going on—" in a politically correct way, of course.

I am viewed as someone who has a seat at the table. As I have grown in my corporate career and begun speaking on more panels about my perspective, it became extremely clear to me that, just like me, there are so many young women who don't know what they don't know. Who, like me, are getting "on the job training" on how to survive as a Black woman in a corporate setting.

Right now, companies have to adhere to Diversity & Inclusion requirements. This means there is a conscious effort to hire a diverse pool of talent in the workplace to create a business advantage thanks to the perspectives of a group of diverse backgrounds and experiences. Consultant group, Global Diversity Practice, explains diversity this way:

Diversity

". . . It's about empowering people by respecting and appreciating what makes them different, in terms of age, gender, ethnicity, religion, disability, sexual orientation, education, and national origin.

Diversity allows for the exploration of these differences in a safe, positive, and nurturing environment. It means understanding one another by surpassing simple tolerance to ensure people truly value their differences. This allows us both to embrace and also to celebrate the rich dimensions of diversity contained within each individual and place positive value on diversity in the community and in the workforce."[1]

Inclusion

"Inclusion is an organizational effort and practices in which different backgrounds are culturally and socially accepted and welcomed, and equally treated. These differences could be self-evident, such as national origin, age, race, and ethnicity, religion/belief, gender, marital status and socioeconomic status or they could be more inherent, such as educational background, training, sector experience, organisational

---

[1] "About: What is Diversity & Inclusion," Global Diversity Practice, https://globaldiversitypractice.com/what-is-diversity-inclusion/.

tenure, even personality, such as introverts and extroverts."[2]

In addition, here are a few statistics to think about:

- Businesses with a healthy balance of men and women are 21% more likely to outperform their competitors.[3]

- Businesses with a good mix of ethnic backgrounds are 33% more likely to outperform their competitors·

- Teams that maintain gender, age, and ethnic diversity make better decisions up to 87% of the time.[4]

So, with proven accounts that companies perform better and have a more competitive edge in their respective markets, what do you think happens? The search begins to meet the quota of diverse candidates and leaders. That's where I enter the picture as what's called a "two-fer." I check two diversity boxes. I kill two birds with one stone. I'm both a minority and a woman. That's the fortunate part about this. The unfortunate part about this is usually when I'm hired, there is a very slim chance another

------

[2] "What is Diversity & Inclusion"

[3] Vivian Hunt et al., "Delivering through Diversity," McKinsey & Company, January 2018, https://www.mckinsey.com/business-functions/organization/our-insights/delivering-through-diversity.

[4] Erik Larson, "New Research: Diversity + Inclusion = Better Decision Making at Work," Forbes, 21 September 2017, https://www.forbes.com/sites/eriklarson/2017/09/21/new-research-diversity-inclusion-better-decision-making-at-work/#77835e84cbfa.

executive who looks like me will get hired also; the quota has been met.

That statement is not meant to be discouraging. I say it to encourage you to start preparing now for when the opportunity presents itself and you become the chosen one. You must make the necessary adjustments and prepare for that moment. You must be ready and fully aware of what's needed to navigate the waters. You must be able to handle the situations presented to you because you have made the right adjustments ahead of time. You must have an understanding of who you are and how you may be viewed when you take your seat at the table. You must clear the path for your career and setup the ball to be spiked at the right time. If your vision is to be the one who is next at the executive level, you must do whatever you need to do to make it happen (within reason, of course).

If from nothing else but my pure experience, I want to share the insights of my journey, a few key points I learned, and the overall value of self-awareness of who you are as a Black woman and how to manage "you" in every possible moment of consciousness. Each page of this book will give you key nuggets to take with you to your team meetings, your after-hours gatherings, your mid-year reviews, and your town hall meetings. I will give you a view of how I started on this path, and what made me realize I wanted to take the road many have traveled but few have made to the end.

In this book, I'm giving you the perspectives I've gained over the years that I figured out by trial and error through my own "on the job training." It wasn't until I got my first executive role that I began to seek mentorship and executive coaching. Before that time, I was literally playing my own personal version of Nintendo's Super Mario Brothers video game with my career; jumping around in unknown territory trying to avoid boulders or jumping into the wrong place, while also trying to collect all the coins and achieve the highest score to win the game. Ironically, if I jumped off the deep end and hypothetically lost a life, somehow, I would pop back up with another opportunity to continue to move forward in a different setting or at a different level, depending on how well I performed.

The secret to a high score in Super Mario Brothers is the same secret to making it to the executive level in corporate America—avoid the turtles (conflicts), dodge the boulders (traps designed for you to fail), and grab as many coins (relationships that support your growth and development) as possible to make it to the next level which is always exponentially harder to achieve than the previous level. Once all levels have been met you can say you have successfully beat the game (made it to the executive level).

This is how it was for me. I jumped in the game and started playing! I didn't have a manual or guidelines that I read prior to putting myself on this path. There was no test of my skill level to validate my qualifications. There was nothing to review – no press briefing before stepping up to the podium. There was nothing. That is why this book is so important. It is my purpose and my goal to provide you with a solid foundation and give you what was an obvious and unidentified deficit for me in my own journey.

I grew up in the sticks of St. Stephen, South Carolina, chewing on sweet grass from my grandmother's front yard, eating rice with every meal, living in a single-wide trailer, making mud pies and running down dirt roads. I've seen an outhouse and actually used one! Right! I've benefited from vacation Bible school and the summer lunch program standing right beside my grandmother Bertha, who was hired to distribute the food to the kids. If I can come from my humble beginnings and climb the corporate ladder with my Christian Louboutin heels on, anyone can do it. My prayer is that sharing the deepest levels of my journey will open your eyes. If at least one minority woman is helped from these "experiences and concepts" I'm about to share, then my ordained mission has been accomplished. Check the box. I'm done!

Introduction

When I think of female executives who inspire me, some of the women who come to mind are the Chairperson and CEO of VEON, member of Uber Board of Directors, and Former Xerox CEO Ursula Burns and the COO of Starbucks and the former President and CEO of Sam's Club, a division of Wal-Mart Stores Inc., Rosalind Brewer. Both of these women exude an iconic quality about themselves that has catapulted them to the C-Suite, a level that many women of color in corporate America only dream of achieving. I look up to them because they have reached the goal I'm preparing to obtain. They are members of a very small and elite group of women of color who are respected and have earned the title as two of the top C-level female executives in the world. They are each notable because, as women of color, they've successfully navigated a unique set of obstacles as they ascended their way up the corporate ladder.

Over the years, I've been honored to hold multiple executive level positions at Fortune 500 companies. As a leader in a tech-based role, I recognize the potential my success has to uplift other women of color and motivate them to aspire to be leaders in the technology industry. Throughout my career, I've continuously set new goals and challenged myself to reach higher levels of influence; viewing my "magical powers" of being an African-American woman as an asset, not an obstacle. Owning the uniqueness of my perspective and understanding the beauty of my differences are what make me a unicorn, that mythical dragon protecting the castle from danger. To know the benefits of being beautiful "twice" is a mental and emotional place that is comfortable and ethereal. I am a woman and I am Black. Most of the time when I'm hired as an executive, I'm usually the only woman of color at that leadership level. Yep, you heard me. I'm usually the only one.

For that reason, I decided to write this book. In a world where companies are screaming the words "diversity and inclusion," there is still a very small number of women of color, specifically Black women, represented at senior executive levels.

Millions of dollars are allocated to support programs that focus on hiring diverse talent, but it seems the impacts are non-existent. With that being said, you must recognize that you are a gift. You bring two very valuable and unique perspectives to the table. You were born with the massive responsibility of positively representing your gender and ethnicity at the same damn time. So, let's talk about what it means to be you! Let's talk about your two perspectives! Let's discuss why what you represent is so desirable and necessary in board rooms. Let's talk about how to become a senior executive and still be your authentic self. Let's talk about why, as a woman of color, you deserve a seat at the table!

At the end of each chapter, there will be two vital points summarizing the purpose for the topic to reiterate the views I want you to take away from the preceding discussion. They are The Gift and The Perspective.

The Gift is exactly what it says–learnings that were ultimately a gift to me that directly or indirectly benefited my career. I've always been told that feedback is a gift and should be used as a benefit, be it positive feedback or constructive criticism regarding areas of improvement and growth opportunities. The Perspective is a summarized account of my view and why I've called out these key points.

I believe the accounts in this book will help open up a different way of thinking for you to navigate to your highest career aspirations while creating a consciousness of who you are as a Black woman in corporate America and what it means to be you. Many of these points may not align with how we think the corporate world should be. I understand that wholeheartedly. However, to win the game, you must first know how to play the game. When you learn how to play the game and win you can subsequently share with others, so you won't always be the only one in the room, and that is how we all change the game for good.

Introduction

As you flip these pages, you will become intimate with some very powerful teachings I've picked up in my career. Great lessons that have helped me understand the importance of embracing who I am, and how to maneuver "me" throughout the corporate climb. It's giving perspective about my journey to becoming an executive as an African-American woman. It's being transparent and sharing the knowledge of what it takes to be on the path to executive leadership without losing who you are. This book will tell you what it means to be in the room, get a seat at the proverbial table, then reconcile how it feels to be the only one.

1
The Journey Begins

"I knew that this was my chance to work hard and set myself up to make a better life for me and my daughter."

My journey has not been traditional by my standards. Yet to others, it may seem like it was done "the right way" and fairly "easy to achieve." There is so much more road for me to travel that I often forget to look back and enjoy the road I have already trekked. The road that brought me to the very spot in which I stand today. That part of my journey is one I need to appreciate more often. Thirty years ago, I did not envision having a corporate career, let alone achieving an executive level title. It was the furthest thought from my mind. My goal was to become a news reporter, be the next Oprah with my own television show, and move to New York City!

I took the train to New York City once I graduated from high school with my dreams and growing fetus in tow. Yes, I was pregnant when I graduated high school, destined to be a teen mom at eighteen years old, but still determined to follow my dream of being a broadcast journalist. I had absolutely no idea how I was going to make it work. I just knew I had to leave the dirt roads of South Carolina if I was to ever have a chance at success. I saw so much for my life and had to figure out how to do it.

I arrived in the borough of Queens, New York to live with my Uncle Willie and his wife Nette, who graciously opened their home to me so I could get on my feet and hopefully start college to study broadcast journalism at St. Johns University. My first job in Queens was working the McDonald's drive thru and dropping fries and pies. After my first few weeks of working, I cashed my paycheck and went to Jamaica Avenue to buy some gold jewelry. You see, back then, in the 80s, having gold chains, door knocker earrings, and bracelets was the style. I had to have some gold jewelry. The next day, I wore ALL my jewelry to work and put it in my locker with no lock on it because I didn't know I needed to lock my locker. You know what happened when I clocked out and went downstairs to gather my things. G-O-N-E, gone! Yep! Every piece of jewelry I bought was gone. I was robbed! Somebody took my shit! My little country self was so naïve, I didn't know any better than to bring all my new jewelry to work. With no lock? GEEZ! It didn't take me long to learn the ways of the city, how to take the bus, keep to myself, and watch my surroundings. The biggest lesson of all: buy a damn lock for my locker!

While all of this was going on, I was still focused on becoming a journalist. That's what I wanted to do, but it became more and more difficult to hide my pregnancy. My belly was growing and it was impossible to hide. One evening, my Uncle came upstairs and told me I had a phone call. My mother was on the other end with a very direct question that I didn't want to answer.

She asked, "Are you pregnant, Monica?"

"Yes," I said.

Her response was, "Okay, you are coming home."

There was no debate. Within a week, I was on my way back to South Carolina and back at home with my parents. My plans had to be adjusted. I was about to become a mother and I knew this was going to change my entire life. My priorities had to change. I still needed an education and I still wanted to be a journalist, but I knew New York had to wait. I had my eye on South Carolina State University and that's where I was going. Close to home with a professional English program AND I could still come home whenever I wanted to. You see, my mother had already told me that I was not staying at home. My parents had agreed to care for my daughter while I was away at school.

After graduating college in 1995, I moved to Atlanta to work for the Atlanta Olympic Broadcast Group (AOB) to support the 1996 Olympic Games. This was my chance, but I was broke as a joke. I was not going to get paid for any work related to the Olympics until after the games ended in August 1996. I had to survive in the meantime. I worked several part-time jobs while I was in training to keep my stomach from singing multiple hunger chords like a Baptist choir. I did what I had to do. I had a roommate to split the bills, worked two part-time jobs, drove a refurbished car given to me by my dad, all while staying focused on doing what I had to do.

Then one Sunday at church (I think), I met someone who worked for Upscale Magazine. I immediately took advantage of the opportunity. I began to network with her and asked if they were hiring for any entry level positions. I remember telling her that I would take any open role available. ANYTHING! I just wanted to get put on and get my toe in the door. A few days later, she called and asked if I would be interested in an administrative position, basically answering the phone and supporting the Editor-in-Chief and all the other writers.

My answer was, "HELL YEAH!"

A whole eight dollars an hour, but I did not care. I took the job! I needed consistent income and this was my opportunity to start building my career. In September of 1995, I began working as an administrative assistant for Upscale Magazine—a well-known publication within the Black community. I knew I would eventually have to tell them about my commitment to the Atlanta Olympic Broadcasting group, but until then, I planned to take the opportunity as far as I could.

I was so thankful for my role as the administrative assistant but I wanted to do more than just answer the phones and open the door for guests. I wanted to write and made my interests known to everyone I spoke with. It was no secret that I had aspirations to be a part of the writing team. I would chat with the other writers, go out to lunch with them, and listen very attentively to the highs and lows of their roles, chiming in with my desires when appropriate. Then, after months and months of reminding the team of my undeniable writing skills, one day I was granted the opportunity to interview Kirk Franklin, who was coming to Atlanta for a gospel concert. We were covering his debut album and tour. Wooo Hooo! I was so excited. Four months later my article was published in the magazine. Don't get it twisted, I was still the admin, BUT I had used my gift of persuasion to finagle a byline on an article in Upscale Magazine.

Soon after that I had to leave Upscale to work for AOB full-time for the 1996 Summer Olympic Games. Upscale was not willing to hold my job until the games ended. I expected that. I left knowing that in three months I would be on the hunt for another job. I was not worried at all and could not focus on what would happen that far in the future. I knew what I had to do and that was enjoy this once in a lifetime opportunity. After the

1996 Summer Olympic Games ended, I was still very focused on my journalism career. So, now what?

Weeks later during a casual conversation with a very close friend from high school, she told me about getting involved in the technology industry. She was a developer already making a significant amount of money as a first-year college graduate. Listening to her was inspiring because my daughter was still away with my parents and I could barely keep the lights on in my current living arrangement. I had no interest in becoming a developer. I was not interested in the tech industry because I didn't really understand it. However, the more we talked about earning potential, the more my interest grew.

I asked her, "What can I do in technology that will let me stay true to my desire to be a journalist and still pay the bills ON TIME?"

Through our dialogue, she told me about a role called technical writer. In the simplest form, someone in the company needed to write the user guides and manuals for the customer service representatives to follow. I could do that easily, earn a few more dollars, and still focus on my journalism career. However, in the quiet and very calculated way that GOD works, the world of technology chose me.

But how did it happen? I mean really, how did I end up with a career in technology when my intentions were to just make a few dollars and bail? When did I decide to make a seemingly temporary decision into a long-term career with more than twenty-five years of experience? In addition, what did I learn along the way that was so helpful? How did I learn that being an African-American woman in corporate America made me different? When reading the words of this book, you will walk away with an understanding of how my life experiences fed my ambition and how my ambition fueled my executive career.

I knew what I wanted for myself and I had to make it happen.

In talking with my friend, I recognized I needed to change my career path. Even though I had embarked on a career in broadcast journalism, after a short time through my stints with Upscale Magazine and AOB, I grasped the understanding that I had to put my journalistic dreams on hold to figure out how to feed my family. Of course, journalism was what I felt I was born to do. Writing and telling compelling stories was, and still is, a passion for me.

Before I made the jump to technology, I began looking into taking my writing skills to television. I thought, "A transition from print to television shouldn't be that hard." But somehow, eight bucks an hour as a "wannabe journalist" became harder and harder to stretch each week. The ability to pay rent, even with a roommate, became more and more difficult. There are only so many times you can call your parents for help and I didn't want to do that anymore. I was a college graduate and should have been able to take care of myself and my oldest daughter. I had to make it work because going back home to the sticks of Stephens was not an option. I repeat: NOT AN OPTION! The decision had to be made. After months of working two retail jobs and days of figuring out how to pay the bills versus which bills could wait, I left the communications field and ventured into technology.

No, I didn't know much about the technology field. My path (I thought) was to be a TV journalist, a correspondent, a news reporter; something that aligned with my love for writing and the arts. However, in talking with my friend, she helped me understand how to translate my skills into a technology role. It was one of the best decisions I've ever made. I knew what I wanted for myself and I had to make it happen. She told me that I could make money doing what I love to do. It sounded like a perfect combination. Sign me up!

This is how my technology career began – by pure happenstance. Who knew one conversation would turn into a life-altering moment? She changed my life forever.

After months of interviewing for different full-time and contracting jobs, I finally got an offer to work for a multinational technology company in their global services department as a technical writer. YES! I secured my first job in the technology field. I was so excited to know that I would actually be able to pay my bills. While not as sexy as writing for a national magazine or hosting a morning news and lifestyle TV show, my hunger to write was fed daily and I was earning three times more money doing it! My hourly rate, you ask? I went from making eight dollars an hour – $16,000 per year salary – to twenty-five dollars an hour, which is the equivalent of $50,000 per year! Wooo freaking Hoooo! It was like an angel came down from heaven with harps playing. Life was so hard and the struggle was even harder.

You see, what I have yet to mention is that somewhere between my move to Atlanta and me trying to make a home with my daughter, she called my father (her grandfather) one day and told him to come get her because she was ready to go home. I was unable to make a home for her at that time. A few days later, my first-born child was back in South Carolina and I was alone in Atlanta trying to figure out how I was going to make it.

At this point, I knew I couldn't lose my new job. I knew that this was my chance to work hard and set myself up to make a better life for me and my daughter. I would do whatever I was asked to do. Working as a technical writer at such a major global technology company would allow me to support my family without worrying about eviction. And while my interest in tech was purely based on the money at first, as I began my journey, I actually began to love what I was doing. It was official. I had been bitten by the tech bug and there was no turning back.

My job as a technical writer was simple—write help desk scripts for the customer service representatives enabling them to support the company's customers. The step-by-step scripts were used to install new products and troubleshoot issues for existing services. The scripts were uploaded into an application and the representatives would use the words that I wrote to help all customers with specific issues.

Easy enough, right? Yes, but there's still a deeper level of the subject matter needed to invoke the ability to listen, understand, and interpret. I had to understand the subject in order to write about it. I knew nothing about technical support, nothing about installing new products, and nothing about troubleshooting issues, but I had no problem learning, either. Mastering this learning curve immediately became a personal challenge because I didn't know the technology industry. I just knew that I had to learn as much as possible to show I could do my job. And so, my journey into corporate America and the tech world began. Changing direction doesn't mean you've failed. It means you are taking an alternate path to success.

The Gift: *Your past circumstances should never have the power to dictate your future outcome!*

The Perspective: *Never be afraid to try something new. You may discover a passion that you never knew existed. Changing direction doesn't mean you've failed, it means you are taking an alternate path to success.*

2

Transformation to Determination

"There isn't one path to get that 'seat at the table,' but there are qualities all executives must possess."

E ach and every day at work as a technical writer became more exciting and challenging. The more I craved knowledge, the more my brain became addicted to problem-solving and figuring things out in a way that could be translated into simpler, easy-to-understand phrases. I began to learn more about the company's products and services because I was writing about those products every day. Not a bad place to be. And it didn't hurt that my first check was triple what I would have made as an entry-level journalist. TRIPLE! Even after taxes.

That's when the shift in my thought process began. I thought:

You mean to tell me that I can make a great salary AND actually have a thriving curiosity and interest in the work I do? Whoa. . . maybe journalism can wait for a minute, at least until I get myself on my feet so I can bring my daughter to Atlanta to live with me.

I thought maybe I could do this tech thing for a few years, save enough money, and use my cushion until I landed my first broadcasting job. But that didn't work out. I thought to myself, *I want to see where this goes.* Working in tech was exciting to me as well as challenging. My brain cannot handle confusion; it's always in a mode where it wants to solve something, learn something, and do something.

My new technical writer role was feeding a need I didn't know I had. Or maybe I knew I had it, but didn't recognize how much the need to learn, lead and grow had to be filled. Given that epiphany, I made a conscious decision to stick with my path and simultaneously decided that I needed to learn more about other roles in the industry. This is where I found out about project management. Once I understood the responsibilities of this role, I loved it and knew it was what I wanted to do. I wanted to lead a team of experts turning a conceptual idea into reality. I had found my target role, the next level, and my inquiring mind wanted to know, *How can I make it happen?*

The saying "closed mouths don't get fed" is so true. I had no problem asking others in the project management roles about how to transition into that position. I was very open with my boss about my new-found interest so he would know I was ready to create a new career path for myself. At the same time, I began to search for another job outside of the company. My strategy: I was going to become a project manager within the company or somewhere else. Either way, it was going to happen. Period!

My first order of business was to update my resumé to reflect tasks and skills related to the project management field. Although I had yet to secure the actual project management title,

I was able to use my writing skills to properly articulate my experience directly related to project management and display how my current job was a one-for-one match to what was required for project managers within an organization. In layman's terms, I reworded my resume to fit the general job description of both a technical writer and project coordinator (entry-level project manager). I knew I could do the job; I just needed a chance. The proverbial foot in the door. I put myself on a path to get to the next level and began to execute those steps each day. I knew what I wanted to do and had no choice but to make it happen.

That meant that I had to focus on what needed to be done in order to have a career in IT (information technology). I became very observant, talked to many different people within the company, and began my relationship-building process. My mission was to learn, understand, and execute. I paid close attention to mannerisms and how other team members interacted with each other in meetings and on conference calls. I did my research on career paths and the qualifications that were needed to qualify for that level. At the same time, I continued to search for another job externally.

In December 1997, I began my second job in the tech industry as a Documentation Lead/Technical Writer for a major telecommunications company on the Customer Operations team and Software Development Center. With this new position, I gained more responsibility and direct interaction with the project management team. I was tasked with creating web pages (something new–yeah!) and updating customer help information.

The section of the website I maintained is where customers could access support information relative to the products and services they received from the company. In addition, the documentation lead role was a key part of the software development lifecycle of work. I was responsible for supporting the project management team in the form of written and online documentation as well as database diagrams.

Database diagrams? That's the job function required to participate in each project assigned to the Software Development center. Taking the Documentation Lead role afforded me a huge opportunity to learn more about project management, the life cycle of software development, the key roles within that process, AND most importantly, an opportunity to network my butt off and build relationships to set myself up for the next jump.

The ironic thing about this strategy is that I didn't realize I was networking and relationship-building until years later. I just knew I had to make things happen, and aligning myself with knowledgeable people seemed like the right thing to do. No one told me this; no one sat me down and gave me the instructions on building relationships, networking, and career management. I had to figure it out. I literally had no choice at this point. My path became my vision for my future. In my mind, it was survival; seeing all the possibilities for my career. The money was great. I needed to take care of my family. I had to do what I had to do and there was no turning back. I didn't know then that what I was doing to network and build relationships was vital to secure support for the next big thing.

My transition into the Information Technology industry happened at a time when there were very few women of color in tech. When I made the decision to pivot, I didn't understand how underrepresented women and women of color were in key technology roles as well as in holding top-level executive leadership positions. But now as I think about it, even if I had known those facts beforehand, they would have served more as motivation for me to disrupt the status quo. I knew my presence in the tech field could have an impact.

It's not hard to notice the lack of diversity in a room of thirty people during JAD (joint application development) sessions, or you're one of a few Black people in the room. JAD sessions were very common in the '90s. All of the key technology solution teams would gather for days in a room to talk about how to develop and deploy the new software and what requirements would turn the concept into an actual product. After days, weeks, or months in a room with the same people, it's not hard to mentally connect with how the room was full of men!

In 2013, the Bureau of Labor Statistics reported that 68 percent of women enroll in college right after high school, yet only 25 percent of these women are represented in the technology field. In addition, studies from the National Center for Women & Information Technology show that African-American women make up only 3 percent of that breakdown. ONLY 3 percent!

Since 1997, I've worked my way up the corporate ladder, holding multiple project management positions, and then moved into leadership roles for national and international companies. After a tenure of just over ten years with the telecommunications company, I was able to move up the ranks to Senior Program Manager.

From Documentation Lead to Senior Program Manager, I was proud of my experiences. I even survived a major company acquisition. I made a lot of traction in ten years from knowing nothing at all about the tech industry to now understanding web development, databases, process flow diagrams, project plans, milestones, data warehousing, and more. I also learned a lot about myself and how to collaborate and influence other people. I learned how to effectively communicate what I'm thinking, write a cohesive response to an email to communicate my thoughts concisely, and interact with others in a team environment. But even thought I'd acquired so much knowledge, I felt stagnant and didn't think there was a chance to be promoted within the company. I was getting the itch again. It was time to move on. At the time, career-pathing was not a consistent topic of discussion like it is now (or should be) in most organizations. Those kinds of conversations were more so approached by the employee instead of the manager. I was the master of my own destiny then just like I am now. Thankfully, there is definitely more focus on growth and development now than there was as I was working my way up the corporate ladder.

I received a call from a recruiter about a job at another communications giant in their Wireless division. The excitement of switching to a new company and learning a new industry was overwhelming. I jumped at the chance. I started as a program manager and then transitioned into a product development role in 2010, overseeing the online help content for self-install customers and working directly with call centers around the world to support our end users. Under the leadership of my new boss, Lewis Simons, I was able to engage in more strategic conversations, learning how to create a vision beyond the obvious to set a plan for execution.

Lewis was the first person to take the time to explain to me what was needed to move from a tactical mindset to a growth mindset. Instead of just looking at tasks and deliverables, he helped me view everything that was being done, and that I was doing in my position, as a part of overall company goals. He was the first person to truly see potential in me and feed that potential with his personal experiences.

Lewis was my first true mentor, and once again, I didn't even recognize what was going on. I didn't know that his stories and Socratic riddles would actually one day make perfect sense. Eventually his teachings all made sense, and to this day, I credit Lewis with being a significant reason for being able to maintain my corporate career.

It was due to his teachings that I was able to successfully move into the next chapter of my career and move into the executive level as a Director of Program Management for a national retail chain. The company has locations servicing the United States, Mexico, and Canada. I was not in the market for a new role at the time. As a matter of fact, I was happy and somewhat content in the product development space and working with the best boss I had ever had! Guess how I found out about the job? THROUGH MY NETWORK!

A call from a college mate and, at the time, Vice President of another tech company was all it took. Trenton Parks reached out to me based on my job experience he'd reviewed on LinkedIn. He called inquiring about my interest, and within the first few minutes of our conversation, he asked me the million-dollar question.

He asked, "Are you willing to relocate?"

My answer was, a resounding, "HELL YEAH!"

His next response was very matter-of-fact. He said, "Okay, if I give them your resume, HR is going to call you based on my referral."

Within two weeks, I was on a plane to New Jersey interviewing with the Vice President of Store Systems and a slew of other people for this director role. After completing interviews with about ten different leaders representing different areas of the company, HR called with an offer for employment. In that moment, my salary doubled, and I officially became an executive in corporate America.

One thing I want to call out here is that I went from a Senior Product Development role straight into leadership. This is not the usual case. Most people believe that you must have a management or senior management title to get to the executive level. While that may be a prerequisite in some organizations, you can see from my experience it is not a necessity, and the kind of corporate jump I made is definitely a possibility.

I have held executive roles at brand name, Fortune 500 companies spanning retail to wireless communications. Those positions led to my role as the former Vice President for a Fortune 1000 streaming service within the Digital Product Development organization.

While the awards and recognition are great, my greatest joy comes from giving back to others coming up behind me, ensuring that I do my due diligence in paving a way for other women of color to acquire leadership roles in corporate America or, better yet, start their own tech companies.

As a woman of color who has successfully broken through many "glass ceilings" and holds a senior leadership title, it's humbling to meet other women of color who aspire to be where I am in my career. One thing I've noticed along my journey, however, is that so many of us have the potential to reach the executive level in our respective fields, but we don't know how to do it or where to start.

I'll be honest – there isn't one path or one method to getting to that seat at the table, but there are certain qualities all executives possess. Those include a determination to transform. Some of these critical transformational qualities may be difficult to teach, but these skills can be realized, guided, and activated with an open and willing participant.

I want to see us climbing the ranks in corporate America and releasing those skills to become the next Ursula Burns or Rosalind Brewer. I will explain to you my "two birds" theory. My theory is based on many companies' desire to kill two birds with one stone by hiring women of color specifically, and how now is the perfect time in history to use that desire to our advantage.

Most importantly, I want to motivate you to crack through those glass ceilings and never look back! I pray that anyone who reads this book gets inspired so you may open your own potential a little bit faster and allow my experience to guide you on your journey to your own seat at the table. It won't be easy, but with your hard work, and most of all confidence in your abilities, you will be able to convince any hiring manager that you deserve that executive role. The future of this world is in the hands of every woman who is ready to lead, and that includes you!

You are the next presidents, vice presidents, and executive leaders of corporate America and NOW is your time to shine. I know you are out there. All it takes is you believing in yourself enough to know that if you see it, you can achieve it.

"Making the choice to build your executive career in corporate America as a minority woman is a major decision."

In 2016 and 2018 respectively, Ursula Burns and Indra Nooyi stepped down from their CEO positions, leaving a huge gap in CEO representation by women of color. In the second quarter of 2019, Mary Winston was appointed the interim CEO for Bed Bath & Beyond. Prior to Mary's recent appointment, there were no African-American women holding the CEO title at a Fortune 500 company. And you know what this means, right? OPPORTUNITY!

Making the choice to build your executive career in corporate America as a minority woman is a major decision. It's a very significant, life-changing path that will take you into rooms you never thought you would walk into and places you never thought you would go. However, this newly-found focus to elevate and move to the next level must come with a high level of self-awareness and the possible obstacles you may face.

There are no written laws that state exactly what you need to do to become the next top-level female executive. If such a thing existed, my story would probably be no different than anyone else's. If there were written instructions and a step-by-step guide, my journey would likely be one that would bore you into a coma. Besides, what's the point of knowing what's going to happen before it happens? It spoils all the fun of living life!

If getting a senior leadership role was a cookie cutter process, there would be many more of us seated at the table. So, let's get down to business and talk about a few key points around what it means to understand who you are as a woman of color on this journey.

It's time to walk into your destiny. It's time to learn how to speak the language. It's time to be okay with focusing on your career moves with very targeted goals and determination. It's time to be comfortable with being confident and not worrying about how your confidence will be viewed by others. Confidence is very attractive!

All you have to do is take a look at each skill you possess, polish them up, smooth out the edges (but not all of them), and reconcile with how important these skills are to your success. As for the ones that are needed but may not be so obvious, we will talk about those skills, too. Once that understanding is met, you will grasp how the dynamics of you as an African-American woman influence the world around you.

> **The Gift:** *As a minority woman, you know how to make things happen. Use your tenacity and creativity to carve out your path to success.*

> **The Perspective:** *You have to understand the rules if you want to win the game. Take the time to learn what is required and double it. You have to work twice as hard to thrive in corporate America; sometimes that's not good enough.*

3
The Dynamics of You

"Now that you've made your decision, you will need to focus on every move you make."

O ne thing I always encourage myself and others that I mentor to do is to make a conscious effort to be self-aware. Understand who you are, how you influence a conversation, and how the dynamics change when you enter a room. Try to connect with what it means to be you. The questions I get asked related to getting promoted and moving up to a higher role are never related to the strategic aspect of the process or understanding the soft skills that are required. A large portion of this dialogue is related to YOU, and about understanding the dynamics of YOU. I've mentored many people over the years. And no matter their age, gender, or where they are in their career, the questions are eerily the same:

> "How can I survive in corporate America without losing my authentic self?"

"I've taken all the training and been here for five years, and I'm still unable to get a promotion!"

"Networking is hard for me. I'd rather just stay away from those events."

"They are not going to promote me because I'm Black."

"Why do I need to play the game? I'm smart and I know what I'm doing."

"Why do I need a mentor? What is the value in having a sponsor and how do I get one?"

All of these questions stem from a lack of self-awareness: not studying the company culture to understand what is important to its leaders, or not understanding your role in recognizing from the outset what the company leadership culture is. There may also be other factors that play into why someone may be stagnant in their role despite multiple attempts to get promoted. Each individual case is different, but there are some fundamental skills to focus on that will give you the tool kit you need to accelerate the process of moving up the ladder by focusing on YOU! Own your authentic self and connect with how that affects every interaction you have.

Self-Awareness

Self-awareness is one of the most important skills you can create and cultivate for your personal and professional career. After reading multiple articles over the years, I can honestly tell you that many people will say they are self-aware when they are not! As a matter of fact, a Harvard Business

Review article found that only 10 to 15 percent of study participants fit the criteria of being self-aware. That's not a large percentage, yet many people fervently believe they are, by all justifications, self-aware. Here is what the Harvard Business Review had to say about the benefits of self-awareness:

> "Research suggests that when we see ourselves clearly, we are more confident and more creative. We make sounder decisions, build stronger relationships, and communicate more effectively. We're less likely to lie, cheat, and steal. We are better workers who get more promotions. And we're more-effective leaders with more-satisfied employees and more-profitable companies."[5]

In addition, most people don't know that there are actually two different kinds of self-awareness—internal and external.

Internal self-awareness speaks to how you see yourself, your values, ambitions, morals, and the way you hold yourself responsible for upholding your values. Basically, it's focusing on you! For example, you know that you don't want to display a certain unfavorable behavior anymore, like cutting someone off mid-sentence. Once you realize this is what you do to most people and you don't want to do that anymore, you are now self-aware of this behavior and you will consciously monitor yourself to ensure that you won't do it anymore. You've become aware of a behavior and you are now holding yourself accountable.

As another example, let's say you are in a relaxed setting with a few of your coworkers and the topic is a project you managed that underperformed and missed a key deadline for the

---

[5] Tasha Eurich, "What Self-Awareness Really Is (and How to Cultivate It)," Harvard Business Review, 4 January 2018, https://hbr.org/2018/01/what-self-awareness-really-is-and-how-to-cultivate-it.

company. Although there were many factors that caused the lapse, you were the person responsible for ensuring an on-time delivery. Most people in the company look at the missed deliverable as being your fault, stating that things should have been done differently. You truly believe you did everything in your power to deliver, but the obstacles were too great to overcome. Every time the project is discussed, you visibly get angry and react negatively to the conversation, speaking in a very forceful tone. I'm sure this is (hopefully) not the way you would prefer to react, but your passion about the topic runs so deep that it's hard to control your reaction until someone in your circle brings it to your attention and shares how difficult it is to deal with you when you are in that state of mind. Now you have become aware of your actions and realize that you do not want to react that way or be viewed as difficult and combative.

This is where the old saying, "when you know better, you do better," comes in to play. You now know what can trigger a negative reaction and that you don't want to display that behavior anymore. So, you begin to work on how you react and hold yourself accountable for handling your triggers in a more professional way. Self-control and accountability for your behavior are key aspects to being internally self-aware. It's not easy to do and takes an open mind, but it's not impossible. Being open enough to admit your own shortcomings is very difficult for almost everyone. But it can be done. Furthermore, internal self-awareness will help you make better decisions about your career based on what you know you want to do.

Next is external self-awareness or, plainly stated, how people see you. The best ways to find out the views of others as they relate to you is to ask and observe. Feedback is a gift. Ask for it. That is the only way you are going to improve and it's the only way you will know how you are doing. However, this only works if the person you are asking feels comfortable enough sharing candid and direct feedback with you. Many people are uncomfortable delivering less-than-favorable feedback, but that shouldn't deter you from asking. Personally, I've never had a problem giving or receiving feedback. It's the gift that keeps on giving. But remember, when you ask for this feedback, you have to be open-minded (referenced above) and ready to receive the feedback without reacting in a negative way if you don't like what you hear. Have self-control.

Writer Caroline Forsey put it like this: "People who know how others see them are typically more empathetic. Leaders who can see how their employees view them are usually more effective, and have stronger relationships with their employees."[6]

As a woman of color, I view being self-aware as a necessity. Dealing with unconscious biases, as well as preconceived and unjustified opinions about who I am throughout my career, I know for sure that understanding who you are, what you value, and connecting with how you influence a room will take you much further than thinking you are the perfect package and no one can tell you anything differently. As women of color, and Black women especially, we already come with labels and expectations about how we will behave. Nobody's perfect, but because there are already thoughts working against us, we have an obligation to ourselves to be accountable for our actions, understand how others see us, and adjust accordingly.

Black Enterprise published a two-part series on this very issue in early 2018 by Michelle Smith, titled "Bringing Your Authentic Self to Work as A Black Woman—Unpacked." The way I see it, there are already several dynamics we have to handle. Having a lack of self-awareness only adds another layer of difficulty to your move up the corporate ladder, and that's not what we want to do. The ultimate goal is to deal with the obstacles we know exist, remove obstacles we've created for ourselves, and prepare our minds to deal with the obstacles we don't know about but will anticipate at some point in our journey.

---

[6] Caroline Forsey, "The True Meaning of Self-Awareness (& How to Tell If You're Actually Self-Aware)," HubSpot, 11 May 2018, https://blog.hubspot.com/marketing/self-awareness.

Emotional Intelligence

This topic is one that I've had to discuss on many occasions, especially as it relates to Black women. Emotional intelligence (EQ) is the management of your emotions and the ability to handle those emotions as a leader. It's a key skill that must be embraced and mastered. With all the other pre-determined obstacles to overcome during the lifecycle of our careers, EQ is a must-have. There is absolutely no way around it.

It's never okay to have an emotional outburst in a corporate setting displaying less-than-cooperative behaviors. Simply speaking, learn to control your emotions! Being professional in all responses at all times gives you a definite lift above your counterparts who are unable to master this skill. It only takes one instance of an uncontrollable reaction to scar your reputation forever! When you enter a room as a Black woman, natural biases will come up whether other people admit it or not.

Cultural biases generate expectations about how Black women behave. Those biases lead to presumptions that we are combative, angry, too assertive, sassy, hard to work with, and extremely emotional. In that moment of boiling feelings, your reaction will make it damn near impossible to get promoted. Your ability to have a disagreeable conversation without being combative will take you much farther than an opposing behavior. You must also have an understanding of the person you are interacting with and how they may perceive you. That level of understanding will give you the ability to adjust what you say and how you deliver the message. The code-switch—we'll get to that in just a moment.

For example, an email your co-worker sent to all of your peers and senior leaders in the organization blaming you for the unfavorable status of the most recent financial report is enough to immediately send you into defense mode. The first reaction to such communication is usually disbelief. Why would they point the finger at you, citing a lack of due diligence in your follow-up as the reason the reports are negative for the month? Once you've accepted the fact that the email will be seen by everyone in your immediate peer group, anger and frustration will soon follow. The best way to handle a situation like this is to walk away for a moment and digest what happened. Calm down.

Think about what you want to achieve by having a conversation with your peer before you respond. Verbally articulate—out loud, and not just in your mind—how you will approach them and connect with your ability to manage your mental and emotional states of mind. Call a mentor or someone you truly respect who can relate and help you talk through your emotions. Have your mentor share examples from their past on how similar scenarios were handled. Whatever you do, find a way to vent outside of the office walls, get your thoughts together, and decide on the most professional way to approach the situation. Do not feed into the angry Black woman stereotype. Always manage your emotions and remain professional. Creating another hurdle for your career is only going to prolong ascending to the next level.

Please understand that becoming emotionally intelligent does not happen overnight. It takes time to understand your own dynamics and how to finesse that understanding throughout your pursuit of a top leadership position. The ability to control a reaction in a matter of seconds, process what is happening to you or around you, and respond accordingly takes focus, a deeper level of self-awareness, and more. Specifically, for women and people of color, the term "emotional intelligence" means a whole lot more. For us, emotional intelligence means survival!

Attorney, Pierre E. Simonvil, very clearly and plainly defines this "survival" as code-switching:

> "More simply put, code switching is what happens when people reflexively or suddenly change the way they express themselves, typically in conformity with

their audience. In practice, this is typically displayed as noticeable changes in attitude, body language and vocabulary depending on environment. Code switching can be as subtle as minor changes in someone's dress and appearance, depending on their environment, or as drastic as a whole personality shifts, with changes in diction and body language."[7]

Code-switching takes a tremendous level of discipline and mental control. I assure you that putting techniques in place like the ones referenced above will ultimately save you from putting an irremovable scar on your corporate transcript. So, let's talk about it.

Code-switching: Do you have to do it?

The practical definition for code-switching according to Oxford University Press, is "to alternate between two or more languages or varieties of language in conversation."[8] However, when put into practice, code-switching is much more burdensome and cumbersome upon the person in its employ.

"While code switching is often viewed as just a nice way people try to bond with others, for many minorities it can become a required survival mechanism in the workplace. Unfortunately for many minorities, particularly blacks and people who come from urban areas, demonstrating their own unique cultural norms

[7] Pierre E. Simonvil, "Code Switching: Does it Help or Hurt Diversity?," New Jersey State Bar Association, February 2019, https://community.njsba.com/blogs/njsba-staff/2019/02/22/code-switching-does-it-help-or-hurt-diversity?ssopc=1.

[8] "Code-Switching," Oxford University Press, 2019, https://www.lexico.com/en/definition/code-switching.

and/or vernacular in the workplace may be fatal to their careers and professional reputation. Which begs the question: is code switching, which in some settings is mandatory, an overall benefit to minorities or good for the promotion of diversity in our society?"[9]

When you think about the above account of code-switching, is it the "overachiever," enhanced version of assimilation? Both assimilation and code-switching have a negative context with code-switching being viewed in the most unfavorable way. If a corporate environment is welcoming of all points of view, all races, all genders, and all ethnicities, would there ever really be a need for code-switching? If there was respect for me as a woman of color, do you think I should ever have to give up who I am to fit in? No, but . . . we have a very long way to go before any person will feel comfortable showing up as their authentic self to the workplace, or in settings where professional colleagues will be present.

Dress the Part: Appearance Does Matter

One thing that will set you apart from the competition is how you present yourself publicly. While your appearance shouldn't matter, the truth is, it does. It's not fair but it's the way it is, so instead of fighting it, why not use that energy to ensure that your appearance reflects the executive leader you desire to become. Besides, you should always want to present your best self at work during this time. There's absolutely nothing wrong with showing your professional style. Through your own observations, you will quickly connect with the acceptable way to dress in your organization. Align with it. You have to dress for the role you want. Once you're established in your executive

---

[9] Simonvil, "Code Switching."

role, then you can begin to tweak the system and put more of your own twist on it.

With that said, you should never feel as though you have to appear in a way that makes you uncomfortable and denies you the ability to express yourself according to the cultural and/or religious standards that are important to you. For example, a Muslim woman should not ever feel like she has to remove her hijab to secure her seat at the table. A Black woman should never feel forced to relax her hair or wear a weave. Forcing anyone to change the essence of their ethnicity, culture, or religious belief is not okay. It is discriminatory and, in some instances, illegal. The advice here is to connect with the environment around you without compromising aspects of your world. Simply put, show that you have a vested interest in being part of the executive team.

As I mentioned earlier, there is a thin line between cultural assimilation and integration. Recognizing that line and doing what makes you feel comfortable is always the best approach. Ultimately, you want to be in the position where a company values you for your intellectual contributions and talents, not your appearance. There is no doubt at all that code-switching can be stressful. It mimics having to live two lives, jumping from your work personality into your authentic self around family and friends. I encourage you to find a workable limit and avoid reaching an extreme state where you completely lose sight of the person you are. Setting your own personal preferences and limits while getting as close to the executive cultural norms without sacrificing your individuality will take time, but you'll get it.

I grew up in a small town in South Carolina with no exposure to the attire of a corporate executive. Most of the people who lived in my hometown were teachers or worked for factories, at the church, or at the local grocery store. My grandmother was the cleaning lady at a local bank where she worked a few evenings each week and took care of me and my cousins during the day. My father worked at the Naval Base in

Charleston, and my mother was a supervisor for the Berkeley County government. All of these jobs are extremely important, but none of them reflected the look of corporate America. Because of this, my attire was casual and bland. I had never been to a big city before moving to Atlanta, which meant that I was green as hell!

I didn't know much about anything and my clothes reflected that. My shoes came from discount stores like Payless or Pic-n-Pay, and I purchased my clothes from stores in Northwoods Mall like Sears and JCPenney. It's not that these stores didn't carry great clothes. I'm sure they did. I just didn't know what to buy that would make me look like I belonged. However, after a few months of working my first corporate tech job, I quickly noticed what people were wearing, especially management. A few of the managers wore business casual attire, but most of them wore suits. The women donned jackets and skirts with heels, while the men wore dark suits and ties almost everyday. My clothes were neat but bland and I wanted to change my look to align more with where I wanted to go in my career versus sticking with the attire for my current role. I began to build a wardrobe more befitting of a top executive. I bought slacks, high-heeled shoes, and suit jackets with my own personal twist to change my daily attire. Doing this gave me the confidence to know that it was just a matter of time before I made it to the next level.

In addition, dressing in a seductive and overly revealing manner is extremely discouraged. As women, we are already dealing with a society that sensationalizes sex all the time. You want to be valued for your intelligence. And, as unfortunate as it is, women have to have a heightened level of consciousness about what we wear to the office. Now there will be exceptions when it won't matter what you have on and you'll have to deal with an inconsiderate jerk who approaches you in an undesirable way. That person must be dealt with immediately and expeditiously. No questions asked! But remember, you have to control the narrative. Understand that what you do, what you say, and how you show up at work will all have an effect on what happens next in your career. Don't give them a reason to hold you back.

Study the Culture, Learn the Language

There is a certain culture that exists in the B- and C-Suites of corporations. This culture is one you should learn and be able to identify in order to secure your seat at the table. Having even a passive interest in golf, for example, can help you hold a conversation with someone in a high-ranking position and may even earn you brownie points when applying for a promotion. You don't have to love the game, but you should know how to play it. Use different tools to your advantage in order to succeed. The phrase "business deals are made on the golf course" is the truth. There are so many articles and numerous studies available that talk about this specific topic. Kristi Dosh wrote about this subject for Forbes in 2016 and found that:

- CEOs who regularly play golf are paid 17% more on average than those who do not.

- A whopping 90% of Fortune 500 CEOs play golf, and 80% of executives say playing golf enables them to establish new business relationships.

- Although only 20% of all golfers are female, 50% of executive women who play golf say being able to talk about golf allows them to be more successful.[10]

---

[10] Kristi Dosh, "Golfers Make Better Business Executives," Forbes, 16 May 2016, https://www.forbes.com/sites/kristidosh/2016/05/16/golfers-make-better-business-executives/#69176bd7b4a5.

For these reasons, I began taking golf lessons in 2015 to gain an advantage in conversations and open up opportunities to be present when these major deals are made. The amount of intimate time spent on the golf course with your boss or the CEO of your company is about four to five hours on average. Those five hours on the links afford you much more time to bond with them and learn more about who they really are. In one game on the green, you can connect with the CEO's executive way of thinking, ask questions about long-term and overall visions for the company, and get a view into how they handle the game of golf.

Do you see an irate reaction when the ball doesn't roll the way they intended? Do they follow the rules? Or are their interactions with the game more laissez-faire and mellow? Whatever experience you have, this time will give you more insight than you could ever get within the walls of your office. I personally wanted to remove as many obstacles as possible and I've always been open to trying new things. So, if something as simple as taking golf lessons could eliminate a hurdle, I was in! AND I actually love playing the game. Imagine that.

While the game of corporate America rarely embraces the culture of women of color, it's important that you're able to identify what is of value to those who are not part of your immediate culture, then use that information to your advantage. This should not be misconstrued as selling out. It's identifying something beyond yourself and your community, then utilizing that "something" as a tool to bring attention to yourself. Then, once all eyes are on you and you've gained your boss's interest, you can show them who YOU are and how you can be an asset in the position you want.

Far too often, we limit ourselves by not attempting to step outside of what we are already accustomed to. You don't have to be a diehard golf enthusiast to be able to have a conversation about it. Think of your passive interest in golf as an icebreaker for potential conversations. You want to have conversations with as many people in the B- and C-suites as possible in order to become a recognizable figure within the company and secure your position at the table.

> **The Gift:** *Don't you ever give them a reason to shut the door on you. Focus on the existing hurdles in front of you without creating new ones.*

> **The Perspective:** *Corporate America has their biased views of minorities, force them to think differently!*

4

You Are Aggressive!
(And Not in a Good Way)

*"Connecting the perspective of others and how you influence a
room is very important because feedback is a gift."*

Dedicating an entire chapter to talk about one word may seem like overkill. However, I want to talk more about just the word "aggressive." It's not so much the word that is the problem, but more so how the word is used depending on the race or gender of the person being addressed. There are varying degrees of meaning and intent when certain words are spoken directly to someone. Depending on the perspective of the speaker and the physical attributes of the person they're speaking to—ultimately, the person receiving the message—one word can trigger either a positive or negative emotional reaction, or influence a change in behavior. If you are a man, you may use certain words to praise or encourage another male colleague who is either a peer or subordinate. However, those same words, when spoken to a woman, may have an entirely different connotation and can be perceived as shaming, shunning, or condemnation. One word that has this double meaning is the word "aggressive."

Words are powerful. Most words have multiple definitions. Let's talk about my favorite descriptor–aggressive. (insert eye roll here). If I had a dollar for every time I heard the phrase, "You are too aggressive," I would have enough money to retire. Ironically, if the same behavior I displayed were showcased by a white male counterpart in the exact same setting, he would be called "assertive" and hailed in a positive light for his persistence. Why are his actions viewed differently? Because he's a white man, and I'm not.

You Are Too Aggressive

Each time I've been reprimanded for my intrusive aggression, my immediate response is, "Thank you for your feedback. Do you have examples of my aggressive behavior?" After an awkward silence of about five to ten seconds, one manager said, "You can't keep steamrolling people. You have to learn how to bring everyone along." Internally, I began my rebuttal, "Who, me? Steamrolling? I'm the most collaborative person on this Earth!" Or at least that's what I thought.

It happened to me in 2017 during my first year as a Senior Director of Program Management at a global content provider. There was a lot happening in the background unbeknownst to me. After learning about the concerns with my leadership, I instantaneously began to self-reflect on what could have caused such a report. I didn't feel like I had done something wrong. I felt that my intentions were totally misunderstood.

You see, this feedback went directly to my boss and I was not given the opportunity to address the concern before it was reported to my leadership. The manager who "told on me" went directly to my boss in tears stating that I was not including her in the conversations to revise the order management process. When actually, it was the polar opposite. She had been invited to all meetings and I even set up one-on-one time with her to set the stage and gather thoughts on the upcoming series of changes. The current process was old, needed to be revamped and was clearly a significant bottleneck to the organization's ability to service customers. For the purpose of this book, I'll call her Marisa.

Marisa was invited to several meetings and only attended one session. As the subject matter expert (SME) and owner of the process, her opinion was required and extremely valuable to the success of piloting the new process. I reached out to her on multiple occasions to explain the mandate from the senior executive team. We met to document the project requirements, and I even talked to her offline a few times to make sure she understood the long-term strategy of the requested change.

Once I had formed the team of experts, the next step was to analyze the end-to-end process, call out pitfalls, and brainstorm on intermediate solutions. Marisa attended the first meeting and then missed every meeting after our first collaborative session. I made attempts to contact her and find out what was going on but got no response. Since we were in different cities, trying to walk by her desk for an ad-hoc face-to-face was not an option. I was left with no choice but to escalate to both her direct manager and to my peer—her director—while asking for an update on the lack of response from their key team member. The deadline to give a readout to the senior leadership team was in jeopardy and I needed details.

A few days later, after an urgent one-on-one meeting was scheduled between Marisa and my boss, it was conveyed to me that my tactics were too much and I needed to temper my aggression. I was confused. The reprimand was unexpected.

Marisa literally cried to our boss about "what I did." Even though I didn't agree with it, I gently nodded, thanked my boss for the feedback, and committed to following up with Marisa to get a deeper understanding of her concern. The biggest thing that really hurt me about this situation was that Marisa was also a Black woman who I was trying my best to help since there were only three of us in the organization and I was the only one at the executive level. As the incomparable Zora Neale Hurston said, "All my skinfolk ain't kinfolk."

When it comes to interacting with other minority women and even Black people as a whole, there is a yearning to uphold the unwritten rule of us looking out for each other. Unfortunately, it hardly ever works out this way. This example only proves that racial and gender biases will supersede the obvious similarities of another woman. Deep down in my heart, I know that Marisa's reaction would have been totally different if she was working with a white man or woman. His actions would have been commended whereas my actions were regarded as intrusive. Connecting the perspectives of others with your influence on a room is very important because feedback is a gift. Being open to views about your performance is never easy, but knowing how others feel about you offers you insight and a perspective you want to remain close to. I've always made a conscious effort to proactively solicit feedback. I don't want to wait to get everything dumped on me in an hour-long performance evaluation. By asking for feedback often, I have had a chance to enhance my good qualities and characteristics, while also focusing on areas of improvement.

But wait, when did being aggressive become a bad thing? Isn't that a desired characteristic when it's time to execute and get shit done? At least, that's what I thought. But that's not always the case. For a woman to be branded as aggressive is like the kiss of death. The same set of traits and indictments that you're constantly dodging as a woman, especially a Black woman, are the same traits that generate praise for your white male counterparts.

I will never be able to hide who I am. When I walk in a room, store, restaurant, or wherever I choose to patronize, anyone with the ability to see will know that I am a Black woman. The course of activities to follow will be a direct reflection of many things—position/title (manager/owner/employee), personal experiences, gender/race biases, childhood teachings, and cultural beliefs.

Here's what I've concluded based on my own personal experience—aggressive or forceful behavior is viewed as a good thing when those actions are displayed by others who don't look like me. Even if I'm responding in an acceptable way, I must articulate my response in a comprehensive manner while tempering my reaction so that it's not received as combative or overly emotional. And even with these adjustments, I may still be labeled "too aggressive" just because of who I am.

It's the hardcore truth. It's unfortunate and a direct reflection of the world we live in today. I would be so excited to report one day that external gender and racial stereotypes were unable to penetrate the walls of every corporation in existence. But that is damn near impossible when, as soon as anyone leaves their office or logs off of the computer for the day, there are many other opportunities to perpetuate racial or gender biases.

Loud. Rude. Aggressive. These words are most commonly used to describe Black women. Stereotypes don't just appear out of nowhere. These words are etched in our DNA at an early age and repeated over and over again.

Federal data from the U.S. Department of Education found school-aged Black girls are taunted for being loud and rude. The data also shows that Black students are still more likely to be suspended from school than their white counterparts, despite there not being any evidence to suggest that they are worse behaved than their white counterparts.[11]

The clouds of aggression or rudeness loom over Black women throughout our entire lives. It's a mental battle that we have to contend with daily. It only becomes more difficult to handle when we are put in the confounding place where we must execute a company's vision but do so in a way that won't offend anyone or piss someone off, since anything we say or do can be misconstrued as being too aggressive.

So, what can be done to eradicate the stereotypes? The reality is it's a constant fight that must always have the full attention of every senior level executive responsible for a diverse pool of employees. If there is ever a chance to change the trajectory of how Black women are treated, supported, and groomed, there must first be a desire to understand the problem followed up by a very actionable plan to fix it and put a solid structure in place to enforce accountability.

You Are Not Aggressive Enough

Comparatively, let's talk about the other side of the spectrum—tempering too much of yourself to the point where your ability to influence is lost due to the fear of you being looked at as the "angry Black woman." I've succumbed to this seemingly corporately-required passivity multiple times. In my reflection, I recognized my own regret for playing small, but was thankful for the lesson at the same time. I learned that I was trying to find what I envisioned as perfection. In my quest to be the "perfect Black corporate woman," I've tread on both sides of being and doing too much and not being or doing enough. It is a

---

[11] "Key Data Highlights on Equity and Opportunity Gaps in our Nation's Public Schools," U.S. Department of Education Office for Civil Rights, 7 June 2016, https://www2.ed.gov/about/offices/list/ocr/docs/2013-14-first-look.pdf.

daily task to find a balance between what is too much and what is not enough.

Each company and organization is different. Regardless, there will always be a need to understand the company culture and how to fit into that environment FIRST! You can begin to influence the organization AFTER you assess what you have to deal with, putting your strategic plan in place to achieve your goals, but I digress.

My first leadership role was with the retail company as Director of Program Management in Union, New Jersey. I was excited, nervous, and doubtful, and I honestly didn't believe I knew what I was doing. However, I must have done something right because I was able to successfully complete over ten interviews and walk away with a job offer. I stayed with the company for three and a half years before moving back to Atlanta because I was homesick and, as a single parent, needed to be closer to my family for support. During one of my final reviews, I received this advice from my boss, the Vice President of Store Systems. She told me to "lead courageously" and never be afraid to speak up.

She said, "You have a lot of valuable experience, Monica. Never be afraid to take ownership."

Those words have stuck with me throughout my career. I was hired for my expertise, but I was scared to be the force in the room because I didn't want to be called aggressive. I didn't want to hear the same things I had heard as a project manager. I did the exact opposite at a time when I should have brought my aggressive-self to the table.

My first leadership role was not the time to be shy, distant, and afraid. I achieved my first executive level status and it was my responsibility to own it. In that moment, my self-awareness grew and my consciousness became elevated. In my mind, I was kicking ass in my position. It wasn't until I received her feedback that I even realized that I had dimmed my talents. For many years, I had to build an ethical reputation of working hard without letting many things, internal or external, hinder my ability to drive teams to complete projects. This was the first time I was told to exist in a way that countered what had been communicated to me in the past. I was given a pass to be myself.

Please understand that both of these scenarios are very stressful. The back-and-forth of trying to decide who you need to be each day as you move from organization to organization, from one leader to another, is like watching a pendulum swing. It also doesn't help that regardless of how magnificent you are or how undeniable your value is, there will eventually be a point where you will have to deal with having the efforts you put forth misinterpreted as aggressive simply because you're a Black woman.

Your responsibility is to always own who you are, then listen, recognize, and use your God-given power of discernment to determine if what you're hearing is coming from a place of elevation or degradation.

Through these experiences, I was able to sharpen my ability to distinguish whether what I was hearing was going to move me forward or hold me back. The aggressive, angry Black woman will consistently live in peoples' minds, but that does not mean that you must accept it as a perfect description of who or what you are. Your awareness will give you the mental and emotional ability to recognize what's going on and handle it in a professional way.

The Gift: *There's a fine line between too much and not enough. That measurement varies with each company. You have to govern your actions and your attitude accordingly.*

The Perspective: *No matter what you say, how you shake a hand or what you do, you will never be perfect. Be okay with that. Somebody is always going to have something to say about you. Use your power of discernment to determine which words are meant to lift you up and which ones are said to bring you down.*

5
Your Network is Your Next Opportunity

"You want to make sure that your professional network reflects who you are AND who you are trying to become."

B uilding and maintaining relationships to support the journey up the ladder is one of the most important aspects of managing your corporate career. The relationships you create will be a stepping stone to achieving higher levels of success. I've met many people over the course of my career. Most of them I've been able to maintain a connection with either via LinkedIn, email, or calling or texting them on the phone. I keep a much smaller subset in constant rotation. This network has become a key aspect of my life that pays priceless dividends over the years. However, this does not extend to all relationships. There are a few people for which we are all better off keeping our distance from. While it would be ideal to stay connected and maintain a professional relationship with everyone, that is not realistic.

For the ones that have longevity, create and maintain a genuine bond that can be leveraged when you're in dire need. It will prove to be more beneficial than randomly submitting your resume for a job through a website. If someone in your network could literally take your resume to the hiring manager of their company along with a personal stamp of approval, the chance of actually getting contacted for an interview increases exponentially. THAT is the power of a network.

Think of your network as opening up a savings account. If you don't make any deposits into the account, there will be no money to withdraw when you need it. The time you spend building relationships and connecting with like-minded people now will pay numerous dividends later. By networking with others inside AND outside of your industry, you create a personal team of colleagues and friends who are more than willing to mentor and support your journey.

Align Yourself with Successful People

I'm sure you've heard the saying that as a professional, you are only as strong as your network. Well, the saying is true. Who you connect with at every stage of your career can be the key to who you become when you're seeking out promotions and new opportunities.

It is important to ensure that your professional circle of colleagues is diverse. You don't want to only associate with people on the same level as you with similar goals. You want to ensure your network includes individuals who are further along in their careers and have reached the level you are seeking to achieve. The goal is to network UP. The only people who can tell you how to get to the next level are the ones who've been there, or are currently holding the title you want.

It's extremely beneficial for you to have a good relationship with individuals who have climbed to the top of the corporate ladder before you. For them, the strategic process of getting promoted has proven to be favorable. The view from the lens of someone who has already arrived at the place you want to go can help pull you up. Their guidance is based on actual tactics that have obviously worked in their favor.

In addition, it is important to have a diverse network of people in your circle. You want to make sure that your professional network and even your personal network reflects who you are and who you are trying to become, certifying that the energy within your various networking circles is positive and reflective of ambitious, like-minded professionals like you. Who you associate with has the power to impact your path, both positively and negatively, and ultimately influence your final destination. The network you choose should consist of people moving in similar directions who are willing to offer perspective to you and receive perspective from you. Remember that your experiences are very valuable and very real. Your perspective can also benefit others around you.

Another component of building a strong network is to join professional organizations. Professional organizations are a great starting point for meeting people within and outside your field, building lifelong connections as you climb up the corporate ladder. Become an active member within these organizations and don't hesitate to take advantage of the relationships you've built. Your visibility within these organizations and the relationship-building opportunities they inherently provide could set you up for the next chapter of your career. The due diligence, passion, and ethics you exude may be just the thing a certain member of the organization needs for his or her new team.

Someone is always watching you. A potential employer having a real example of your ability to perform, handle pressure, and collaborate with others is all that is needed to onboard their team. Oftentimes, the final decision of who gets a particular position relies on **who** you know and not **what** you know. Positioning yourself to know more people of influence will prove to be significantly advantageous to your career.

The Information Technology Senior Management Forum, more affectionately known as ITSMF, was the first professional organization I joined specifically for the purpose of networking and creating alliances to support the upward ascension of my career. Ironically, I was introduced to ITSMF by someone in my network. Four times a year, the organization convenes at different locations across the United States to bond, share viewpoints on various topics, and, guess what, NETWORK! The first symposium I attended was in June 2013 in Atlanta, Georgia.

The mission of ITSMF is:

> "ITSMF increases the representation of Black professionals at senior levels in technology, to impact organizational innovation and growth. We do this by developing and nurturing these dynamic leaders through enrichment of the mind, body and soul."[12]

WOW! This mission statement spoke to me when I first became introduced to ITSMF. It was exactly what I needed, and because I was still in my first role as an executive, I became even more magnetically attracted to this organization. After attending my first event, I was hooked. I completed my application for membership a few months later and received my acceptance in November. The friends I've made and the relationships I've built through ITSMF have all exceeded my expectations. Aligning with Chief Information Officers, Vice Presidents, and successful entrepreneurs who look like me gave me the additional inspiration and drive I needed to continue with my personal goal to become a high-ranking Black female executive. ITSMF

---

[12] "About: Our Mission," Information Technology Management Forum, 2017, https://itsmfonline.org/about-itsmf/.

became my toolkit for awareness, guidance, and perseverance. They are my extended family!

Now is a very opportune time to be a woman of color in business. As discussions surrounding equal pay, diversity, and inclusion continue to trend socially and politically in America, now is the perfect time to use your intersectionality to your advantage. This is a moment in history when women, specifically women of color, are the most educated and business-oriented demographic in the country. Companies are seeking a way to capitalize off of our expertise for their corporate benefit.

Some hiring managers and recruiters across the country are actively seeking out talent among women of color to meet diversity requirements by killing "two birds with one stone." From a public relations point of view, it is ideal to showcase a diverse and inclusive group of people amongst a leadership team. The good thing about this hiring strategy is that opportunities have opened up for bad ass Black women to fill. Adversely, once the diversity requirement has been met, it is highly unlikely that another Black woman—or more broadly, another minority—will get hired after her. After both boxes have been checked, the corporate mentality has been, "Let's move on."

Online Networking Is Critical

Many professional networking sites available boast that their platform can provide the biggest return on your investment. Standing in the spotlight as the behemoth of all professional platforms is LinkedIn. As of the first quarter of 2020, LinkedIn's reported membership is at 610 million people around the world, and the number keeps growing.

Maintaining an up-to-date profile on LinkedIn is an absolute requirement when trying to present your background, education, and talents to a pool of potential employers. Personally, I have been contacted by executive recruiters on many different occasions via LinkedIn to discuss potential job opportunities purely based on my profile. One such conversation actually turned into a job offer.

After two years as a Director of Program Management for a wireless communications company, I was informed by my senior director that my job was being relocated back to Seattle. I was given the option to move to Washington and keep my job or remain in Atlanta and accept the severance package. This happened in September 2017. I had just relocated back to Atlanta a few years prior and I was not interested in moving my entire family to Seattle. I'm definitely an advocate for relocating for the right role, but living on the west coast was not appealing to me. I happily accepted the severance package with the clear understanding that I did not have another job lined up. That meant that I had to begin the search for the next big thing.

The first action item was to check my LinkedIn for accuracy, certifying there were no typos or grammatical errors, and that the summaries conveyed the message of an experienced, strategic senior executive. I also upgraded my profile to the premium package to increase my visibility among recruiters, and to see the number of profile views I was receiving along with other analytical data. Then I changed the setting on my profile to "yes" to let recruiters know that I was interested in new opportunities. That way, if my profile was viewed by someone scanning the site for qualified candidates, it would be known that I am open to the conversation. Checking, updating, and networking through LinkedIn became a daily responsibility to support the quest for a new position.

Next, I contacted many of my technology friends, senior executives and recruiting companies within my network to let them know I was seeking a new opportunity. I sent them my updated resume and requested lunch/dinner meetings with anyone who was available to meet with me. They were all helpful and did not hesitate to offer the influence of their own personal network to support my efforts.

This is the same network I spent years building, and as I said earlier, it was paying back in massive dividends! My network proved to be rock solid and aside from just making me feel great, it gave me confidence that it would not be long before I had secured another leadership role. Working both my online presence through LinkedIn and my personal connections gave me an advantage over others who had not dedicated the time to invest in building a long-lasting pipeline of professional support.

A few weeks into my job search, I applied for an Executive Director role with the business side of a cable company through LinkedIn. The recruiter for the job contacted me a few days later to schedule time for an initial discussion about the role and confirm the job was a good fit for me, and that I was still interested in pursuing the role.

We met the next day via conference call and I was moved to the next round of interviews without hesitation. Twelve interviews and two months later, I received a job offer to join the team as the Executive Director for Program Management for a cable company. This role was a promotion. I received a salary increase, more responsibility, and a larger team to manage all while working for well-recognized Fortune 50 brand. I learned about the job via LinkedIn. With this job, same as many of the other positions I've held in the past, I was the only Black female executive at or above the director level within the organization. The only one!

Avoid Social Media Pitfalls

Social media is a phenomenal way to connect with friends, meet new people, and even run an online business. Twitter, Instagram, Facebook, Snapchat, and a host of other interactive platforms are used for a myriad of reasons. Most people use social media to show aspects of their personal and professional lives. By putting personal events on a public stage, it's easy for anyone, even hiring managers and recruiters, to see what you've posted on your pages. A few words of advice if you want to be viewed and hired as a top-level executive—be careful of what you post on your page!

Yes, it's your page, but please be mindful that whatever you post could reflect negatively on you, and therefore will reflect negatively on the company's brand if you are hired. Many companies are now reviewing social media as a way to determine if you are a good fit. They need to know that you embody the morals and values that align with their brand.

As a senior executive, you will be one of the faces representing the leadership team on stage during town hall meetings, high-profile meetings, and in external publications. Vulgarities, explicit, or revealing photos or videos, fighting, or anything that is unfavorable to your personal brand and damaging to your reputation should never, ever be made available for public consumption. That behavior may work for others in different industries, but it will not work for you in corporate America.

There are already many stereotypes to contend with as a Black woman. Adding to the list of obstacles by what you choose to display on your chosen social media platforms is deeply discouraged. Don't do it! You must hold yourself to a higher standard at all times. Before you post a picture or video to your social media pages, ask yourself this one question: "Could this damage my chances of getting hired?"

If the answer is yes, don't post it. If you are unsure, don't post it. Technically, if you even have to ask the question, chances are you shouldn't post it. Period!

Mentorship

Mentoring is so important to me that I have decided to leave you with this message. As you have seen, there are so many things to consider when planning and executing your rise to the top of the corporate ladder. But what good is it to learn from your experiences and grow as a leader if you don't have time to reach back and bring others with you? I mean, that's the only way the number of Black executives will increase. For me, mentoring is two-fold—sharing my experience with other rising executives and having the blessed opportunity to spend time with top-minority executives who feed off the knowledge given to me. I have an obligation to mentor others any way I can. As a Black woman, I have a responsibility to do what I can to prepare the next generation of Black female leaders.

Honestly, in the early days of my career, I didn't even know I needed a mentor, let alone understand the multifaceted benefits of having one. Having a mentor was the best-kept secret that wasn't even a secret. No one ever told me about this goodness.

You mean I can align myself with others who've already walked this path and they can guide me by sharing their experiences with ME?

WHO KNEW!

Thinking back, I had my first mentor when I was an individual contributor at a communications company. As I mentioned in Chapter 2, my boss, Lewis Simons, was very insightful and often pulled me in his office to "explain" what just happened in a meeting we attended. He was very specific about the dynamics of the room, key influencers, and why things were said in a certain way. He would often use his whiteboard to help clarify strategic terms and share his thoughts while asking me to interpret (regurgitate) what he said with my own twist to confirm I understood. I didn't always get it right, but what he did single-handedly changed the trajectory of my career. From that role, I was able to interview for a director-level position AND GET IT!

I went from an individual contributor straight to a director, skipping the management levels in between. WHOA! The crazy thing about this scenario is that I didn't even realize how unusual it was until years later. My boss was my mentor. He changed my thought from tactical to strategic. Meaning I was more focused on the tasks that needed to be done (tactical) versus understanding how the completion of those tasks would impact the company's goals (strategic). He helped me understand how to be present in the proverbial room. He challenged me to think beyond the task in front of me. I am thankful to him for seeing potential in me when I didn't know a greater ME existed. Lewis kick-started my executive career. His mentoring prepared me for the leap I took which secured my first director role and literally changed the course of my career path.

I highly recommend securing a mentor, if not two or three who represent different views. They don't have to come from the same industry, but as you can see, having a mentor can have a huge influence on your corporate journey.

Set up frequent discussions either on the phone, video chat, or face-to-face. The goal is to learn as much as possible, storing each nugget in your toolkit to be used along the way. The mentor-mentee relationship should be mutually beneficial, but primarily beneficial to you. If you feel that the relationship is not working well, don't be afraid to cut your losses and move on to another mentor. There is no law that says you have to stay with a particular person. Keep going until you find the right one. You will know if a mentor is right for you when conversations feel natural and comfortable. Interactions will be seamless. Great mentor/mentee relationships will prove to be beneficial in a short time through meaningful insights relevant to your current situations. Conversations that feel forced, robotic, or strained make it difficult to create a natural bond with your mentor. Infrequent touch points coupled with the feeling that there's a lack of interest in connecting with you is a very good chance that you need to find another mentor. Everyone's time is precious, and when you see signs that show a lack of interest in helping you, don't be afraid to move on.

Sponsorship

When I speak of getting a sponsor, I'm not referring to just anyone within your current circle or at your current job.

Honestly, a sponsor can and should come directly from your network. I'm referring to an influential professional who is willing to put their reputation on the line to represent OR recommend you to others with hiring potential. A sponsor is the person who speaks on your behalf when you are not in the room. Your sponsor will always have your best interest in mind and the ability to move you up the ladder a little faster. They will not hesitate to help you if they are in the position to do so. You do not select a sponsor; a sponsor selects you!

This does not mean that you should befriend someone specifically for this purpose. The key word is "genuine." The sponsor is there to be a helping hand and catalyst for your career, representing you in conversations and places you have yet to gain access. When someone decides to sponsor you, please DO NOT TAKE IT LIGHTLY! Becoming your sponsor means that they trust your work ethic, professionalism, and character. If you were to secure a job simply by having them represent you, your obligation is to kick ass and be the best damn executive ever hired.

You are a reflection of your sponsor's brand. Being unappreciative, having sloppy work performance, or being unprofessional is the quickest way to lose your job AND lose your sponsor forever. Trust me. I've never lost a sponsor but I've seen it happen to others. It is so important to treat your professional network with unwavering gratitude and appreciation. All of the people you know can easily spend their precious time building the brand of someone else. If you are the one they choose to bond with, be grateful. You need all the help, support, and encouragement you can get.

The Gift: *A truly solid network willingly gives everything it has to offer. You have to take the time to grow it and appreciate its value!*

The Perspective: *I learned everything about career management on my own. Any opportunity to avoid making mistakes — take it! Your network is that opportunity!*

6
Characteristics of a *Bad Ass* Executive

"Leaders are able to see the larger picture and how each decision affects the company at both a macro- and micro-level."

E veryone is looking for the magic combination of words and skills to create a cookie-cutter mold that could make anyone an instant executive. If that were possible, the mold would be applied to all people and fit all organizations. I wish it were that simple, but it's not. The truth is there are basic skills and characteristics commonly found in most leaders.

Companies in the market for top-tier executives are looking for the person who can position their organization to have a larger competitive edge, gain more market share, exponentially grow a business arm of the company, and/or maintain the business in an underperforming economy.

Whatever the reason, the skills needed to achieve the company's goal will be the focus of the executive search.

During my mentoring sessions, I talk about recent events in my mentees' professional careers and tie them back to how they can achieve a different level of strategic thought and business acumen from a particular incident. It's building leadership muscle through a true connection that will never be forgotten, forcing my mentees to open their eyes and be more conscious of what's happening to them and around them. Real examples assist with pinpointing moments to enhance emotional intelligence and their ability to influence an organization.

So, what are the skills that small and large corporations need to trust you with to lead a core, multi-million-dollar business function, or the most profitable and high-profile division of the company? These critical skills you will need in order to be distinguished as a *bad ass* executive include:

1. Executive Presence
2. Strong Communication Skills
3. Ability to Build Relationships
4. Innovative Mindset
5. People-first Leadership Style

Executive Presence

Executive presence is a set of qualities almost every leader of a corporation personifies. It is the fuel that propels them to the top of their fields and the essence of who they are as professionals. If I were to create a recipe for the most important traits that embody executive presence, the recipe would start with a one-third cup of confidence, a one-third cup of composure, and a one-third cup of resilience. Each of the aforementioned ingredients are equally important, and when mixed together, creates one powerful executive who can lead ANY company to achieve their goals.

A leader with executive presence is recognized immediately. The mere entrance of a person into a conference room or even a casual setting sets him or her apart from everyone else. Executives who embody all three of the aforementioned traits remove all doubt about who is in charge. The confidence is validated by body language such as good posture, leaning into the table, keeping the body open (not crossing arms), and eye contact. It's in your attitude and your conversation. Confidence is everything. Additionally, being well-dressed is another way confidence is enhanced because when you look good, you feel good. A well put-together appearance is attractive to the eye regardless of whether it's a casual setting or in the office.

We talked about dressing the part in chapter three, so now you know your appearance is equally important to endorse your executive presence. Confidence is how you solidify that you belong in the room with everyone else. If you don't believe you deserve to be there way deep down in the pit of your belly, I guarantee you no one else will believe it either. And very soon, the blood, sweat, and tears used to get the seat at the table will soon be lost to you and go to someone else.

Secondly, maintaining your composure in the middle of a crisis and making sound decisions while under extreme pressure is another way leaders personify executive presence. The ability to think clearly during a chaotic situation is tough but it has to be done. Holding top tier positions comes with a lot of stress that must be managed well when people are in a state of worry, concern, anger, and fear. Others around you may not be able to compose themselves during this time, but YOU have no choice but to keep your emotions in check. Remain poised, focused on the end goal, and mentally balanced. Times like these have the propensity to create imbalance which will inhibit clear decision-making requirements.

The final key point is resilience. Resilience speaks to the capability to bounce back quickly. Are you able to take a professional hit to the chest, absorb the blow, and recover within seconds, ready and prepared for when it happens again? Yes, you are!

For example, let's say your current assignment is to oversee the development of the number one project in the company. Most of the fiscal budget has been allocated to fund this project and the new product features are viewed as the holy grail of technology. This project—let's call it Project Destiny—would be the industry differentiator everyone in the company has been waiting for. You attend all the meetings to get a real time update on progress and all reports have been good. That is until a meeting is scheduled to talk about a drastic twist of events causing massive delays to Project Destiny. The project has been delayed for reasons outside of your control but YOU are responsible for ensuring the work is completed on-time. How would you explain the delay to the C-Suite executives and other stakeholders as well as convey messaging about the delay to trade publications?

A blow like this could be career-ending. Project delays will always and forever equate to an increased budget and asking for more money, and it is not a fun conversation to have. Learning of delays to projects with high visibility that are out of your control is hard, but you have to bounce back from the news quickly. No matter the amount of "what ifs" or "have we tried this" questions asked, the reality is a hit like this requires an explanation and fast! What happened and why wasn't the problem mitigated sooner? What is the plan to fix it?

Being able to take a major hit and still shine in the end is the epitome of resilience. You have to have a huge reserve of resilience to be a top-ranking executive. Therefore, fail fast, learn quickly from major mistakes or setbacks, and keep it moving.

Strong Communication Skills

Never underestimate how critical it is to verbally articulate and physically translate your thoughts with clarity and enthusiasm to your leadership team, peers, and direct reports in your organization. Writing an email, speaking at a company-wide town hall meeting, putting together a PowerPoint presentation, or even adding verbiage to explain a quarterly report are just a few responsibilities requiring the ability to turn your thoughts into comprehensible, easily-digested exposition.

There will be many times when you will have to address the entire company via email or on stage. Simple things like capitalizations, subject-verb agreement, broken sentences, and choppy thoughts while speaking will significantly diminish the effectiveness of the message and potentially damage your credibility as a leader worthy to run a company. Those missteps are a distraction and it is very difficult for your team, peers, and the C-level executive team to connect with a message no one can understand. Remember, as women of color, we are held to a higher standard of execution. In most cases, delivering an incomprehensible message will be unforgivable.

I would highly recommend putting a couple of checkpoints in place that will absolutely help you slam dunk your verbal and written communications each time. The first thing to do when you know you have to speak on a particular topic in a company-wide setting is write down your key points and potential take aways. Transcribing thoughts from brain to paper is the first and most important step to communication. Doing this forces you to mentally connect with the message you want to deliver. Also, knowing your audience and what you want them to take away will help you anticipate their questions so you can proactively address as many topics as possible with your message. Write it down!

The second checkpoint is practice, practice, practice. FaceTime a friend and ask them to give you candid feedback. Solicit your family's participation by asking them to sit down on the couch to listen to your presentation. Since they don't work with you every day, they will have no clue about the topic of discussion. When you are done, ask them if they connected with the key points conveyed. I'm sure you will get some very honest feedback from them. If their answer is yes with head nods around the room, job well done. If they didn't understand anything you said, that means there may be more work to be done. You can also use someone you trust within the organization and get their opinion as well. The viewpoint from an internal colleague is a great way to confirm you have connected the dots in a way that will resonate with everyone.

Relationship Building

It's important to realize that building solid relationships you can leverage throughout your tenure at a company or even along the way of your career is proven to be one of the leading characteristics of a successful executive. There is no way around it. Having leverage by way of relationship-building creates a sense of loyalty, mutual understanding, respect, and trust. Even though developing alliances with as many people as possible is always good, pay close attention to the folks who are considered "influencers." These are the people who can change the minds of everyone in a meeting by only making a few statements because of their trusted viewpoint and solid reputation.

The influencer is the person who can walk into the CEO's office and get exactly what they ask for with minimal hesitation. The influencer has immediate name recognition, which comes in handy if there's ever a need to name-drop. An influencer can be a developer, a senior manager who's been with the company for fifteen years, or even the executive assistant. When it's time to get the work done and there are roadblocks that need to be removed, your relationships can be used to keep the momentum going.

Relationship-building also applies to interactions with clients, strategic partners, as well as your team of direct reports. This is a core competency for all executives, and a very critical pillar to uphold a well-respected reputation as a leader who values what others can bring to the table. You are not in this alone. Furthermore, neither individual nor company success can be achieved without relationship building. We are all dependent upon each other to manifest the company's vision. With that being said, it is imperative to spend time grooming and growing as many relationships as you can. It is literally impossible to be successful without them.

The best way to build mutually beneficial relationships will differ from person to person. Things like organizational culture, individual personalities, and confidence levels will affect the approach. However, I truly believe that going back to the basic way of initiating conversation is the most effective.

For example, extend an invitation to lunch or drinks after work (your treat) to someone you'd like to get to know better on the professional level. Set up a fifteen-minute meeting to introduce and talk about how you can assist with a new project assignment. Grab their attention by saying hello as you pass each other in the hallway, then strike up a conversation and ask for permission to follow up with a more in-depth discussion at a later time. Use this time to learn about their personal interests outside of the office, their family, and even their hobbies. You may learn that you have several things in common with them. The point is, you need to hone in on the commonalities between the two of you and then expand the conversation into an invitation to meet again.

Consider these suggested conversation starters:

"You're a golfer, too? Let's get together next weekend and play a few rounds."

"I'm a member of a group that mentors teenage girls interested in corporate careers. I'd love to have you come by and speak to them about your experiences."

"My daughter's dance school is amazing! Since you're looking for a school, I'll give you the studio's information and call them to give my personal recommendation."

If getting together externally is not an option, set up a time to meet in a conference room, the office common area, or in the bistro down the hall. The bottom line is the importance of relationship-building is immeasurable and the benefits will far exceed the time spent setting a solid foundation for future collaborations and alliances. In this corporate game, with the obstacles already in place, you will need all the help you can get.

Innovative Mindset: Thinking Outside of the Box

An innovative mindset can be defined as thinking outside of the box; solving a future problem before it exists and forming an environment that encourages and appreciates new ideas. One of the biggest responsibilities you will have in every leadership position is to be a catalyst for change. When you are hired, part of your role is to implement fresh and improved ways to enhance a product's performance, implement a new service to fill an industry gap, or be the first to market with a groundbreaking concept.

Top-tier executives are often visionaries who see boundless potential for their company, constantly planning for ways to expand the company's brand, extend their reach beyond perceived barriers, and most importantly, increase the bottom line. The best leaders are always thinking of new ways to grow revenue, market share, or build industry partnerships. The quest to be the industry pioneer will never fade, and as you climb the corporate ladder to your own executive level position, you will have a significant role in making that happen.

To feed and grow an innovative mindset, consider the following points.

Know Your Industry

Read trade magazines, online articles, and government publications, and attend conferences to attach yourself to the latest industry trends. Do whatever it takes to get smart as fast as you can within your chosen industry. An in-depth understanding of where and how your industry trends are moving is the springboard to the creative process.

Know Your Competitors

Positioning the organization to get a competitive edge takes a lot work. It requires the study of any public information about your competitors' fiscal strengths and weaknesses, researching rumors of new product offerings as well as understanding profitable signature features.

Know Your Customers

While analyzing your competitors' performance, there should also be a focus on your company's performance. What is your current ranking in the market? What are strategic ways to enhance the customer experience and increase profitability at the same time? The answer to that question lies with your customers. Ask them. Soliciting feedback from active customers is the fastest way to know if you are doing a great job or if you have blind spots that need to be immediately addressed.

Know Your Organization

All this talk about innovation and new ideas is truly awesome. The cultural infrastructure is there; you've opened up the minds of everyone around you to "think outside the box." Now what? Do you have the right processes in place to effectively iterate and deliver a new product or service quickly? An exciting idea has been reviewed and approved—do you have the right skill set on the floor to start development work? Historically, what has been the success rate of previous projects? The capacity to deliver is equally as important as creating an incubator for new ideas. One cannot survive without the other.

Now that you have a better understanding of how to adapt your mindset, use this knowledge as a tool to differentiate yourself and your company by challenging current habits that may be inhibiting progress. Continuous encouragement to look beyond the obvious is necessary to becoming the number one contender for the position you want. An innovative mindset is essential if you are going to lead your team to greatness.

When you and your team make the decision to implement a new idea, it's time to get moving. This is where "leading courageously" steps in again. Risk is inevitable. Doing something different that may test the comfort level of others around you will require a lot of courage. Most people have a low tolerance for risk, which is the antithesis of an innovative mindset. You have to speak life into the vision. Your passion and support is all the motivation others need in order to get aligned and on board. Will there be naysayers? Of course. A good mix of supporters and haters is to be expected no matter what you do. Managing your response to be positive and forward-thinking is how you gain the buy-in of everyone who will be involved or impacted by the project. Innovation is the lifeline of a cutting-edge team and it is your mandated duty to bring forth new concepts, openly solicit innovative thoughts from your team, and happily accept the challenge to be the catalyst for change.

People-First Leadership Style: Empathy

Corporate entities are the sum of the people employed by the company. All of us are human beings who have lives outside of the office. Personally, leading an organization with a people-first mindset is THE MOST IMPORTANT characteristic to me according to my personal leadership style. Empathetic leadership is viewed as one of the top five core competencies of a great leader, oftentimes referred to as number one on the list.

What is the definition of an empathetic leader? Executives with a high propensity for empathy are concerned about employee experiences and care about their opinions and perspective. Most of the time, empathy is described as being soft and easy to persuade. Weak. In fact, it's just the opposite. It doesn't take much effort to care about your own thoughts and opinions, but how effective is that going to be if you have no clue how your team feels about what is happening around them? Showing care and concern creates a loyal team that would do whatever is needed to solidify success—theirs and yours.

Empathetic leaders are also very encouraging and motivating. These leaders are genuinely excited about individual progress while encouraging an entire organization to reach its potential. You need them more than they need you. So, why not take the time to connect with the perspective of your team? You will gain the superhero powers of trust, loyalty, and unfiltered insights as well as an unwavering dedication to you with every conversation you have with people on your team and in the company at large.

Tim Stobierski writes, "Your ability, as a manager, to understand the emotions that your team members are feeling allows you not only to become a more effective communicator and problem solver, but also to build the rapport, trust, and relationships that fuel team success."[13]

Similarly, Development Dimensions International found that empathy was the number one skill for overall success:

"There is one leadership skill that ranks far and above all others in determining your overall success as a

---

[13] Tim Stobierski, "How to Become a More Empathetic Leader," Northeastern University, 2 August 2018, https://www.northeastern.edu/graduate/blog/become-an-empathetic-leader/.

leader . . . Leaders who master listening and responding with empathy will perform more than 40 percent higher in overall performance, coaching, engaging others, planning and organizing, and decision making, according to the research."[14]

Recently, an employee from my team called to say that her mother was only given a few days to live and she had to leave the very next morning to fly to India. She sent an email to me and her direct manager with all of her project contacts and the latest status update for each one. Her mother passed away within a week of her arrival. The family was devastated and so was she, but she still tried to continue working while she was taking care of her mother's personal business in India. She had no idea when she would be ready to return to the U.S. I immediately set up a meeting with her manager to discuss options for support during her time of bereavement. The very next day, I sent her an email telling her to stop working and to take care of her family. I also committed to working with her on the HR process as needed, keeping her main focus on her family.

At the time, I was the Vice President of the company. But here I was taking notes, running project meetings, and following up on action items. At that moment, my VP title did not matter! If the tables were turned, I would want that same courtesy extended to me.

A month later, the employee returned to her home in California and set up a meeting with me the next day just to say THANK YOU! The fact that she didn't have to worry about work while she was with her family meant so much to her. She said that there were not enough words to explain the level of gratitude. At the end of the day, that's what empathetic

---

[14] Evan Sinar, Ph.D. et al, "What's the Number 1 Leadership Skill for Overall Success?," Developmental Dimensions International, 23, February 2016, https://www.ddiworld.com/global-offices/united-states/press-room/what-is-the-1-leadership-skill-for-overall-success.

leadership is all about. The work will always be there, but work should never, ever take the place of time with your family or personal priorities. Do unto others as you would have them do unto you. (It's the golden rule for a reason.)

My empathy level is elevated. I've had many different experiences that evoked deep and scarring pits of emotion. I have been judged based on race and gender, treated unfairly because my boss or my peers didn't agree with my leadership style, and blatantly interrupted in meetings as if I wasn't speaking at all. I have been shunned because I have spoken up too much or not enough, called out on behaviors that would have been rewarded if done by my white male counterparts, and had my ambition questioned condescendingly by other Black colleagues telling me, "You won't get promoted," or, "They will let you in because they like you."

I understand how it feels to be overlooked and ignored. I feel, on a visceral level, the pain of being challenged or demeaned simply because of who I am. However, if it were not for these experiences, I would not be able to extend the same grace to others I wish had been given to me. This grace, this empathy, is what sets me apart, and when it comes to finding leaders, separating the empathic is the first step to promoting you above your peers.

The Gift: *The breakdown of these five core leadership competencies is the blueprint to position you for executive royalty!*

The Perspective: *I will never forget to be a human first! Caring for the team is a sign of strength and courage, not weakness.*

7

Hire One, Get One Free

"The concept of getting a two-for-one deal unconditionally applies when I'm hired as an executive."

Shopping is a concept everyone is familiar with. The concept of exchanging currency for goods or services dates back thousands of years. Almost everything in this world has some sort of monetary value attached to it. Some things are more expensive than others. Therefore, any opportunity to get more value for less money is excessively appealing. Retailers often use the concept of "BOGO—buy one, get one free" to entice customers to buy more products, tempting them with the chance to pay less money but get more value with their purchase.

This is how I feel about being hired as a Black woman in corporate America. Of course, I'm not technically being bought and traded (that's illegal), but the concept of getting a two-for-one deal unconditionally applies when I'm hired as an executive who just happens to qualify for two diversity checks—I'm a woman and I'm Black! Relating to the extreme focus corporations are supposed to have when it comes to hiring a diverse pool of candidates, I qualify to check two diversity boxes.

The exciting part about this is that any opportunity to increase the pipeline of diverse leaders in a company deserves to be celebrated. These types of hires are scarce, and since the occurrences of these hires are few and far between, every victory must be flaunted and celebrated. Adversely, at the time I'm writing this book, it's devastating to know that the number of minority CEOs continues to dwindle to its lowest point in almost 20 years.

Right now there are only four Black CEOs running Fortune 500 companies. They are Kenneth Frazier, who oversees Merck & Co., a pharmaceutical company. Marvin Ellison is the CEO of the big box home improvement store, Lowe's. Jide Zeitlen is the CEO of Tapestry, a fashion holding company. Finally, Roger Ferguson, Jr. is the CEO of TIAA, a banking and insurance company. Do you see a trend here?

At the time of this book's publication, the only Black CEOs of Fortune 500 companies are men. Meanwhile, only two Black women have ever led an S&P 500 company. The first is Ursula Burns, who served as the CEO of Xerox from 2009 to 2016. The second is Mary Winston, who served as the interim CEO of Bed Bath & Beyond for six months in 2019.

These numbers are disheartening, but not discouraging. I have no choice but to believe that the perspective of corporate America will soon change and the momentum will once again start to move upward. I'm committed to doing whatever I can to influence the trajectory of opportunities for women of color, especially Black women! My obligation includes this book, mentoring, speaking on panels to bring attention to the issue, and outwardly advocating for diversity and inclusion wherever I'm employed. I've made it a personal charge to upwardly spike the curve.

Even though there is an obvious representation gap at the CEO level, there are other C-level roles where women are increasingly being hired. Chief Human Resource officers have more women leading organizations than all other C-level titles. But the role is held by mostly white women.[15] Chief Marketing Officers (CMO), Chief Financial Officers (CFO) and Chief Information Officers (CIO) have all experienced an increase in female representation,[16] but Black female incumbents in these roles are still very low.[17]

Why is this still true? Are the two diversity checks for the price of one no longer attractive? Let's explore a few points influencing the increase in representation of Black women in top level positions.

Intersectionality Invisibility

The practical definition of intersectionality is the theory that the overlap of various social identities, such as race, gender, sexuality, and class, contributes to the specific type of systemic oppression and discrimination experienced by an individual. The term was originally coined in 1989 by Black feminist scholar, lawyer, and UCLA law professor Kimberlé Williams Crenshaw.

---

[15] Anne Stych, "HR Professionsals are Overwhelmingly White," *The Business Journals*, 27 February 2019, https://www.bizjournals.com/bizwomen/news/latest-news/2019/02/hr-professionals-are-overwhelmingly-white-women.html

[16] Anne Stych, "Percentage of Women in C-Suite Roles Inching Up," *The Business Journals*, 24 April 2019, https://www.bizjournals.com/bizwomen/news/latest-news/2019/04/percentage-of-women-in-c-suite-roles-inching-up.html?page=all

[17] Alexis Nicole Smith et al., "Interviews with 59 Black Female Executives Explore Intersectional Invisibility and Strategies to Overcome It," *Harvard Business Review*, 10 May 2018, https://hbr.org/2018/05/interviews-with-59-black-female-executives-explore-intersectional-invisibility-and-strategies-to-overcome-it

Invisibility comes into play when intersectional social identities are used to purposefully overlook individuals and invoke discriminatory action. In this way, intersectionality invisibility directly applies to Black women. It's one of the many hurdles we have to jump during the race to the top. Our presence is obvious in rooms where minority women are underrepresented, but by contrast, our characteristics of gender and ethnicity are used to marginalize our opinion and diminish our validity as often as possible. Intersectionality invisibility is exactly why we have to work twice as hard to be seen, respected, and viewed as a valued part of the team.

Living in a world of intersectionality is hard. Trying to navigate the waters in the skin I'm in comes with challenges, uncertainties, and daily insecurities. Things like how much of a Black girl can I be today? Is it too much? Do I pull back and fade into the background? Is blending in not enough? How will I be judged? I think about it each time I walk into the office or join a video call, carefully articulating my words for fear of sounding uneducated or being perceived as such. Should I share details about my life or limit those conversations to my family and friends because getting too close means getting too comfortable and *we know* I'm not allowed to get too comfortable? Every aspect of who I am requires a decision as it relates to how I show up in my executive role. The decisions I make determine how I will be judged and the fear of judgement fuels these insecurities.

"Who am I going to be today?" It's a question I'm confronted with every day as a Black female executive in corporate America. The person I pick to show up as on any given day always has genuine intentions to avoid intersectionality and marginalization as much as possible. I want to show up in a way where I can just be without having to worry about my God-given features as Black, or female, being used against me. But is it even possible to present myself in a way that all unconscious biases are forgotten? NO! There will always be thought or action to contend with regardless of how hard I try to eliminate biases through my interactions.

The adage I live by is, "Life is 10 percent what happens to you and 90 percent how you react to it!"

No matter what happens to me resulting from preconceived notions that are outside of my control, I will always remain professional and poised. Reacting irrationally and allowing emotions to prevail over judgment is relinquishing control. No one is worthy of having that level of control over me. For this reason alone, I made a commitment to myself to always maintain control of my emotions (emotional intelligence), and to evaluate the person I bring to the table on any given day (self-awareness).

The Spotlight Syndrome : "Look, we got one!"

Spotlight Syndrome is a term I coined to describe what happens too often when the "two for the price of one" hire has been made. You have now become the face for the brochure, the trophy on display. The company's work is done, and there's no need to do any more.

"We got our two-for-one! Woot woot!"

Because you have checked the two diversity boxes for executive level representation, the likelihood of another Black female leader being hired is ultimately nonexistent. I wish it were not true, but from my own experience, the number of people of color, let alone women, who were hired at the executive level after me in companies where I worked is a whopping zero. My counteraction to this practice is to fully embrace my new-found position as an opportunity to praise the efforts of a company that proactively chose to focus on diverse hiring, while at the same time, shedding a light on the need to continue to search for and hire other qualified, diverse talent. If an organization stops at one diverse executive hire thinking that

Hire One, Get One Free

is enough, there are serious issues with the mindset of the senior leaders.

Building alliances with key influencers is the most effective way to become part of the cataclysmic movement for change. The first thing I like to do is align with my HR partners to engage in open dialogue about how I can support more diverse hiring practices. Everything from reviewing interview questions for potential biases to analyzing the percentage of diverse employees being promoted are just a couple of ways to ensure each person is getting a fair chance at being considered for higher level roles. Next, I try to find out about active employee resource groups (ERGs) to become a member or executive sponsor, graciously offering my support to the cause.

In my previous role as Vice President of Program Management for a global streaming service, I was the only Black female on the product development organization's leadership team. When I started, it was obvious that the boss was proud of the hire. As I understood the recruiting process, the mandate was to find a Black female to fill the role based in Atlanta. I made this conclusion because I knew of two other women who had been contacted for the same role and both of them were—you guessed it—Black. That mandate obviously played in my favor because after several interviews and a flight to Oakland, I received a job offer to join the leadership team.

Once again, I was the only minority female executive on the team. I noticed right away that there was no hesitation to put that fact on display. It was a familiar place for me but, for this particular role, the focus seemed to be elevated. Spotlight Syndrome was in effect. My name was referenced during several town hall meetings, and I was given a topic to present at several of those meetings. I could be wrong and maybe even slightly paranoid at this point in my career. Maybe it was my fair shake and my chance to represent myself as a leader. Maybe not. Regardless of the intent, I embraced the chance to be the face for company leadership in Atlanta and beyond. Shedding light on my status as the only Black female leader within the product development team by accepting speaking engagements and participating in events enhanced the awareness of diversity and inclusion company-wide. Instead of running from the spotlight, I used it as the springboard to expedite change.

Shortly after joining the company, I was asked by multiple local employee resource groups to be their executive sponsor. I was honored to sponsor multiple areas doing whatever I could to support events related to diversity and inclusion. As the only minority face on the leadership team, there was extreme interest in enlisting me as an advisory partner of the ERGs.

By default, the only Black female in position tends to become the chosen one to represent all Black women. This is a perfect example of why when "the one" gets hired, it's imperative to open doors for others using the "spotlight" to positively influence more diverse hiring practices.

Witnessing behaviors of unfavorable hiring practices should trigger an innate desire to change what's happening in front of you. When this happens, you may be blinded by the spotlight shining in your direction. Instead of looking at it from a place of vexation, twist it into a chance to steer the organization into a positive direction. Create opportunities for other Black women to get hired. Checking two diversity boxes is not the equivalent of one and done. More of us must be pulled up the rungs of the ladder. Right now, if one of us is hired to check the gender and race boxes at the executive level, it can be expected that our hire will satisfy the requirement and that no one else will get in. Using the Spotlight Syndrome to positively impact the view of Black women and increase the pipeline of diverse talent is not an option; it's an obligation.

Women of Color vs. Black Women

Let's be clear—I may use the phrases "women of color" and "Black women" interchangeably in this book. However, they are by no means exactly the same. The phrase "women of color" is inclusive of all women who identify as non-white. Latina, Asian, Indian, etc. are all classified as women of color. Saying "Black women" is more direct. There is no question of gender or ethnicity when the phrase "Black women" is uttered. Lumping all non-white women in to one category is not ideal. Pairing the story of Black women with other ethnicities washes out our story and cancels the uniqueness of our perspective. The experiences of Black women yield a different return than that of my Latina or Asian counterparts. I have much love for my minority sisters, but there is an immense difference between my view of the world and theirs. The plight of Black women requires targeted emphasis to correct in corporate America. Being lumped into one category with all other minority women has not helped us at all. It creates a deeper level of marginalization that we cannot afford to have. Our story is different from other minority women.

Black women are looked upon differently than all other races or ethnicities of women. I've mentioned this fact a few times and it's worthy of reiterating often. We have to contend with being perceived as angry all the time, combative, sassy, and difficult to work with. Coupled with evidence from many research studies that we are paid significantly less than our white counterparts, it is evident that we fall last in the hierarchy of privilege. Here's the order of earning potential from highest to lowest purely based on ethnicity and gender: White Men, White Women, Black Men, Black Women. Additionally, LatinX men and women fall behind Black women with an even larger pay gap, making only fifty-five cents on the dollar.

Our experience is less valued and our intersectionality only aids to deepen the gap. The Joint Economic Committee of The United States Congress released a report in 2016 stating that "women of color face even larger gender pay gaps. Compared to white men, African-American women, on average, are paid only 60 cents on the dollar..."[18] Yet the study goes on to find that "Asian women face the smallest gap relative to white men, earning 84 percent of white men's earnings." On average, Asian women are paid more than a Black woman. An Asian woman is considered a woman of color, but as you can see, our story is different from other minority women. I'll dive deeper into compensation gaps in the next chapter, but for now, know that the wage gap and the proliferation of equal paydays created to bring attention to the issue is another intersectional battle Black women must contend with.

Inequalities are commonplace for Black women to experience in the corporate setting. They stem from hundreds of years of institutionalized racism and being told that as women, we are second class citizens only good enough to clean homes and make babies. Our battles are not equal to that of other minority women who have their own obstacles to face. While I respect the journey and setbacks we all have to overcome, my eyes will never be able to look through their lenses. Only through empathy and the experiences from my own path can I connect with other women, but being part of a larger group diminishes the relevance of the Black female experience. All of the various ethnic groups have commonalities, but as Black women, our story will always and forever be different from any other group of minority women.

---

[18] Joint Economic Committee United States Congress, "Gender Pay Inequality: Consequences for Women, Families and the Economy," A Report by the Joint Economic Committee Democratic Staff, April 2016, https://www.jec.senate.gov/public/_cache/files/0779dc2f-4a4e-4386-b847-9ae919735acc/gender-pay-inequality----us-congress-joint-economic-committee.pdf

The Gift: *Your complexity as a Black woman is what makes you unique. Embrace it and use every situation to shine a light on your greatness!*

The Perspective: *Use every opportunity you can to move from invisible to visible. Your past will lay the foundation for your future.*

8

Recognize the "It" in You

"You've invested a lot of time in managing your career and you deserve to be in the room."

Becoming a top-level executive and joining the leadership team of a Fortune 500 corporation is not impossible—I am living proof. But the reality is, there are necessary steps required to secure a place at the top. You have to master the most sought-after leadership skills and maintain a solid network of influential relationships. Additionally, with the right amount of self-reflection, ambition, and perseverance, you must understand the depths of who you are and exude confidence in everything you do.

Entering a room with your head up and shoulders back is not cliché. It's the body language that lets you and everyone else know that you belong. It's a true sign of confidence. A strong handshake, direct eye contact, or a subtle smile are physical attributes that outwardly emote the confidence inside. This is the point when you no longer have to convince yourself of your capabilities because you believe in them. Confidence is another superpower. Your confidence in yourself directly correlates to the confidence others will have in you. Once that superpower is at full strength, no one will be able to stop you from accomplishing your goals.

There is no doubt in my mind that as women, we have the traits that can lead each of us into a successful career. The components outlined in this book bring to the forefront critical characteristics you need to have the awareness necessary to conquer the many obstacles you will face in a professional way. Don't allow those obstacles to force you to give up or stray off course. Will you doubt yourself at some point? Yes. Will you be 100 percent fearless the entire time? No, no one can be fearless all the time; it's human nature. During those moments when you feel discouraged, frustrated, or defeated, allow yourself to be vulnerable and feel the pain. Then, use the memory of that feeling as fuel to boost your ambition and keep going. Rely on your confidence and strength.

You've invested a lot of time in managing your career and you deserve to be in the room. Know your worth! You want to achieve professional goals and lead multi-million dollar and even billion dollar corporations, right? Remain confident and resilient and persevere. By simply embracing the concept that you belong and you're just as worthy as everyone else will give you a sense of purpose that will spill over into your interview process, salary negotiations, decision making ability, and handling of crucial conversations in highly stressful situations.

Listen, I get it. All of this sounds easier said than done. I'm not trying to make light of what is required to play this game of corporate chess. It's tough. Really tough. There are so many aspects to consider—physical attributes, racism, gender biases, classism, body language, mental and emotional strength, what you wear, knowing how others see you, how you view yourself, what's too much, what's not enough . . . UGGHH! It's a lot to consume. I know.

The fact that you are reading this book right now lets me know that you are already committed to refining the path forward to move closer to your goals. You're headed in the right direction with the right mindset to get the job done. Designing your own personal blueprint for success and committing fully to achieving your goals will no doubt get you to the top. Learning the rules of the corporate game will set you up to win the game. Be patient but diligent, and most importantly, believe in your achievements and know that, without a doubt, you are worthy and you belong at the table.

Know Your Worth

As I briefly mentioned in the preceding chapter, there continues to be a huge gap in salary compensation between men and women. Women in general are not paid anywhere near their white male counterparts in corporate America. The disparities in salary are just as significant for the general category of women of color, but the gap is even worse for Black women. The salary gap is so pervasive that there are now laws in place for several states prohibiting employers from inquiring about compensation history. The law was put into place solely to support efforts to close the compensation gap.

It starts with the first job. At the time of hire, you probably are not aware that you are underpaid. The pride and excitement of securing your first job is overwhelming. You show up to work day after day feeling proud of your achievement and ready to work harder than everyone around you. That is until you somehow find out that the salary for one of your male peers is higher than yours. Whether someone informs you at a happy hour after a few drinks or in the common area for lunch where others are listening attentively to the office gossip, regardless of how the message is delivered, curiosity will soon take over. It may be hard to validate the exact number (then again, maybe not, depending on who you know–friends in management or HR, hint hint), but the fact is, there may be some truth in what you hear.

Consequently, let's say what you heard is true, and your peer, let's call him Bret, makes about 15K more than you. When Bret leaves his current role and gets another job, he will take his 15K advantage with him and will potentially get an additional 10K bump in salary with his new job. A few months later, you also decide to leave the company for a new role and you also receive a 10K bump in salary. But guess what? You are still making LESS THAN your former colleague, even though both of you got the exact same amount of increased salary. THIS is the problem that continues to compound over the years, making it damn near impossible to catch up with your male counterparts. No matter how many promotions you get, you will always be behind the curve in comparison to white men.

For this reason, seventeen states in the U.S. have enacted legislation to eliminate the need to validate salary history. This sets the stage for women to be compensated based on their experience instead of institutionalized racial or gender predispositions. Furthermore, seventeen cities have also aligned with the ban and two states have countered the legislative ban by allowing employers to request historic salary information.[19] Those two states are Michigan and Wisconsin. Where you live or the state where you intend to work may determine your ability to close the pay gap that is based on gender, race, and ethnicity biases.

This is the time to do your research. Websites like Salary, Glassdoor, and Indeed.com are phenomenal resources to get details on the average compensation range for certain roles. Use these sites to enhance your negotiation skills by walking in an interview fully informed about salary expectations. Once again quoting the Joint Economic Congress report, Black women are often subjected to a racial and gender pay gap. The

---

[19] "Your Guide to Salary History Laws by State and Locality," *Salary*, 2020, https://www.salary.com/resources/guides/salary-history-inquiry-bans/

fact that Black women are only paid an average of 60 cents for every dollar a white man makes directly sheds light on the reality that our fight for equal pay is difficult.

So, how do you demand what you're worth when it's a national issue, you may ask? You must get smart average salary requirements for the role you are seeking and never be afraid to advocate for yourself. This is also a perfect opportunity to leverage your network and solicit candid information about salary bands within their organizations. Having a direct connection to the hiring managers will give you unfiltered access to a wealth of compensation information. Reach out to a few of your mentors to gain insight on how the pay grades within their organizations work and tips on how to communicate your salary expectations. Valuable information is right at your fingertips when you leverage your network.

This inside industry knowledge positions you to start with an enormous advantage when it's time for salary negotiations. The path to resolve this racial/gender pay gap is incredibly hard, but strides can be made one person at a time. In addition to doing research before the interview, I've used the following tactics to help me negotiate every dollar I can BEFORE I EVER accept a job offer.

Do Your Research

This is worth stating multiple times. If you don't know the market demands for your skillset, how can you effectively determine your worth?

Pay Attention

Pay close attention to the interviewer's tone and body language during interviews. Use that strategic muscle to start the chess game. You'll quickly be able to determine the next move based on the response.

Speak With Authority

Put some bass in your voice. I know that may sound like a joke, but seriously, it is not the time to be timid, shy, or unsure of yourself when asking for more money. Lack of confidence is easy to detect and the wrong person will quickly pounce on that insecurity and use it as a tactic to manipulate the conversation. Take the time to role play with your mentor or a close friend to become comfortable with having the money conversation. Your confidence, or lack thereof, will cost you dearly in the end.

Know When to Stop

I'm sure you've heard to never accept the first offer, and I wholeheartedly agree with that. Take a day or two to review the offer and then come back with a counter. Leverage your network (again) and talk to others to find out if the offer is fair, then make adjustments to push the envelope a bit. Write down the details of the counter offer, then submit it to the employer for review. If the offer is accepted, YAY! If the counter is rejected and the initial offer stands, you then have to make a decision about whether you want to keep pushing. My advice is, at this point, to take the offer if it meets your expectations. Or, decline the offer and keep it moving. Make the best decision for you!

To close the gap and boldly approach the topic of money requires you to flirt with the risk of being labeled as aggressive. I'm sorry, it's going to happen whether you agree with it or not. Be firm, be confident, but be mindful that the person on the other side of the table from you during the salary negotiation will always have an opinion about you, making their own conclusion about whether you are being aggressive (not in a good way) with your ask for equal pay solely because of who you are. Regardless of the national issue surrounding the wage gap, you have to make it clear that you deserve equal pay. Any traction you make during the negotiation process to increase your yearly income coupled with benefits and incentives is a big win!

Lean in Without Fear

For such a small word, fear has the eminent power to inhibit life-changing decisions. From a young age, we are raised to be the foundation for our life partners and family. Young girls are rarely encouraged to be bold and take charge even though we are already born with that burning desire to lead.

One phrase I remember being told is, "It's better to be seen and not heard. Little girls are not loud."

Well, why not? I want to be heard, too. Statements like that repeated over and over again to very impressionable little girls can subconsciously create a fear of standing out that innately manifests itself with age. We then question our ability to succeed. Is it okay to take control of a situation? Am I being too aggressive? There goes that word again.

Childhood events can carry deep scars and create fears that are difficult to overcome as an adult when it's time to make a decision that will change the course of the rest of your life. What do you have to lose by leaning in without fear of the consequences? You're afraid to ask for a raise, huh? Why? Scared of losing your job? Your boss may get upset with you? What happens if you actually ask for a raise and get it? Imagine that. You overcome the fear of losing your job AND you actually get a bump in compensation for not being afraid to lean in. YOU WIN!

For me, my stubbornness and ambition proved to be more powerful than any childhood edict. I don't have to be quiet. I want to be seen and heard, and I'm not afraid to say it. My ambition drove me to set goals for my career and achieve them. My stubbornness does not allow me to take no for an answer. I didn't know what I was doing; I just knew I had to excel, and I did it.

Understanding how fear influences decision-making abilities requires a deep sense of self-awareness. Fear creates doubt and doubt creates apprehension. Lots of "what ifs" come into play. Consider the following examples.

"I want to take on a new project, but what if she says no?"

"What if I ask for a promotion and I don't get it?"

Well, you may actually get promoted if you ask! Isn't the promotion what you wanted all along? And because you were not afraid to ask, your desire became a reality. Bottom line is you will never know until you become confident enough to stand in your truth without fear as a barrier, step into your greatness, and ask for what you deserve.

As women, we hold ourselves to a very high standard of accountability. Basically, if a woman is going to dedicate time to do a newly-assigned initiative, she's going all in. But this mindset of being perfect and "all in" has proven to be a hindrance as well. Studies have shown that job-seeking women will read a job description and won't submit their resume because they may be deficient in one or two of the requested skills because of minimal experience or no experience in that particular area at all. Studies show that we have to have everything in place before making a move, such as checking ALL the requirements listed for the job and not just a majority of them. The working thought is that because we don't meet all the requirements, we are not good enough to get the job done and done well. This is a lack of confidence. It's the fear of failure.

Men, on the other hand, will apply for a job with only 60 percent of the qualifications because they believe that their majority experience is just as good as the woman waiting for the 100 percent. There is no innate fear in men that they won't be successful. Most men are fearless when it's time to manage their corporate career.

The truth is, your current experience level and background is more probably more than enough to be successful and to do the job exceedingly well. Furthermore, what you don't have in your background you can learn as an active part of your new job.

The emotional tax we have to pay as women working for a corporation is extremely high. There is already a shortage of Black women climbing the higher rungs of the corporate ladder. We must take on the personal responsibility of being fearless and unafraid to be present, and command what we deserve to be paid. Doing this would be a great start to removing fear and replacing it with confidence and balance.

Advocate for Yourself (Celebrate You)

"If you don't celebrate you, no one else will."

These words were uttered to me by one of my mentors in 2016. I had just received the Women of Color STEM Conference Special Recognition Award and I didn't want to post anything about it for fear (we just talked about fear) of sounding like I was bragging about my achievements. She was right. Nobody called me to ask if it was okay to post my award on their social media or professional website. Nobody is going to do that. Why would they? Most people are too busy spotlighting their own accomplishments which leaves no time to talk about yours. Actually, it's not someone else's job to celebrate your professional accolades; that job is 100 percent yours.

Early on, I was never a person to talk about my achievements or name drop in every sentence to get attention. It was unnecessary for me to focus on such things. I didn't need to boast about what I'd done. My fear (that word again) of sounding braggadocious made me stray completely away from any type of post to bring my achievements to the forefront of the minds of everyone who happens to follow me or be friends with me online. But then my mentor said, "It's not bragging if it's a fact."

That statement was a home-run for me, in that it instantly encouraged me to be proud of myself. The lightbulb was on. From that point forward, I always made a point to celebrate my accomplishments and be proud of my success.

Sharing my story also helps to bring awareness to so many people and inspires countless others who may see me on my journey and change the course of their career just by looking at my path. There aren't many of us in this race, but having an identifiable face could be all that's needed to get other Black women to aspire toward an executive career in technology.

Remember, it's not bragging if it's the truth. Share your story, inspire others, and be proud of what you've done.

> **The Gift**: *You are just as good if not better. You belong in the room. You belong at the table. Step in with confidence. Command what you deserve.*

> **The Perspective**: *Your perspective and your experience are extremely valuable assets and different from everyone else. If you don't know your worth, no one else will, so don't expect anyone to see what you don't see in yourself.*

9
Everything You Do Matters

"There's a strategy that accompanies job performance and career advancement. It's the politics of it all."

It may be a hard concept to grasp, but it's true—everything you do matters when you have made the choice to focus on elevating your executive career. When you are in the vicinity of your peers and leadership, be mindful of what you say and who you say it to. A relaxed environment with colleagues from work, either at a restaurant or an unrelated gathering of friends, may fool you into thinking that it's okay to jump into a conversation bashing a fellow co-worker or your boss. It's very easy to get comfortable, especially after a few glasses of Caymus Vineyards Special Selection Cabernet Sauvignon (my personal preference). Anyway, never, ever let your guard down too much. Establish your personal limits and boundaries and stick to them. No matter how much you've bonded with a co-worker, you should not let it all hang out! NOT EVER!

Personal feelings about office affairs are just that, personal, and personal is where those opinions belong. A casual conversation about how much you dislike your boss or how your peer only got the job because of his dad's relationship with the CEO can be misconstrued and exaggerated. Unless you are 1000 percent sure you can trust the receiver, keep your thoughts to yourself. Whatever you say or do will be a discussion topic the next day at work and for days, even years, to come. The very words you speak aloud can be used against you. Don't say anything that has the potential to damage your path forward. No matter what you are told by your peers or colleagues, never let your guard down. I mean never!

This order of behavior carries over into your actions. What you say and what you do are all closely monitored once your career aspirations are known (especially by others), and sometimes, it can take years before you realize that people are keeping tabs on your behavior—words and actions—to either help or harm you as you move forward on your career path. People pay close attention to body language, facial expressions, intonations, breathing patterns, eye contact, and your interactions with everyone around you. There are mental journals created with your name on it, equipped with dates, times, and sprinkled with a bit of personal interpretation.

You must quickly connect with the fact that what happens in Vegas never stays in Vegas! Vegas rules do not apply to the corporate game. So, when you get sloppy drunk at the holiday party or you match the banter of a brash team member by openly arguing about recommendations to solve an extremely important issue, each scenario becomes a journal entry in the book of "you" that will never be forgotten. At any given moment, that journal will be opened and used, and it will be to your disadvantage. As I've stated before, don't give anyone a reason to hold you back.

All Eyes On You!

The paranoia that accompanies knowing that you are constantly being watched can be comforting to those seeking the attention and scary to others who believe that the amount of surveillance is a high price to pay to be promoted. It doesn't matter which side you're most comfortable with—someone is watching you, and it's the price you have to pay. Period. It is unreasonable to believe that on your upward career journey no one is paying attention to you. How else will your manager be able to measure your level of readiness for more responsibilities if they're not watching and assessing your current abilities and potential capabilities? Use this time on stage to showcase collaboration, decision making, and communication skills. Present the best, most-qualified "you" every chance you get. At the same time, be honest about skills that require you to grow. Acknowledging areas of deficiency is a sign of strength and self-awareness, which are both attractive traits of a leader.

The *All Eyez On Me* double album was released in 1996 by the legendary musician and philanthropist Tupac Amaru Shakur. The title song, while filled with expletives and imagery of a less than desirable and unchosen thug life, summarizes his need to protect himself and how he lived every day in constant fear for his life because people were watching his every move out of jealousy, which was a consequence of his success. Why was he being watched? Well, he was famous. Tupac's undeniable talent separated him from the general population. When Tupac became famous, the whole world began watching him.

Fame is a glaring spotlight that separates the known from the unknown. Fame creates focus, intrigue, adoration, jealousy and disdain. You will experience a smaller variation of this as you move through your corporate career, but it's all relative. Tupac had the eyes of millions of fans watching him. Your company will have hundreds, maybe even thousands of people watching you. When you are positioning yourself as having "next" (getting a promotion or moving up in your corporate career), doubters will be intrigued to know how you got to the point where you are, and why you are excelling over them. Supporters will show adoration by cheering you on hoping you get what you deserve, and the haters will inevitably show jealousy by planting seeds of discouragement and discontent.

The amount of focus will also be unjustly elevated because you are a Black woman or woman of color bearing twice the burden and overcoming twice as many obstructions than any other demographic. The goal here is for you to understand what is happening around you (lots of people are watching you), why it's happening (you stand out more than anyone else), and what to do when it happens (take advantage of both the good and the bad).

Drinking in Work Environments

In the early 2000s, I attended a technology conference in Orlando, Florida. I hadn't attended many conferences, so of course I was excited to travel on the company's dime. The day we arrived, we all decided to check into our rooms and meet up later at the hotel bar for a few drinks. I agreed to convene with them, and a few hours later we were all at the bar drinking cocktails, listening to '80s pop music and enjoying a few greasy appetizers. A couple hours later, one of my co-workers had consumed his share of gin and tonics. So much so, that when we all decided it was time to get some rest and prepare for our early start the next day, he was unable to get out of his seat and stand up straight.

He acknowledged his first stumble by quickly attempting to reassure us that he was okay and throwing his hand up. His second stumble landed him on the floor only seconds after he tried to tell us that he was alright. I was embarrassed as if I was the person that fell down. We all rallied around him to get him up off the floor helping him balance his stance enough to walk toward the elevator and then to his room. After a male colleague volunteered to ensure his safe arrival to his room, we all dispersed for the evening.

How many drinks did I have that night? One glass of wine and a glass of water. That's it! My co-worker's behavior that evening solidified the reason why I control the amount of alcohol I consume in the presence of other co-workers. My white male co-worker felt that it was okay to be inebriated in a business setting. The likelihood of him experiencing backlash for being drunk is nonexistent. It was clear he did not care about the perception of his image. He got drunk, fell down, and didn't have a care in the world the next day. He only talked about how he had such a great time.

On the other hand, I know that if that had been me stumbling around in a drunken stupor, falling all over the place, the news of my behavior would have made it back to Atlanta before sunrise. For us, this type of sin is unforgivable and will never be forgotten. Our threshold for imperfection is shallow and our rope is short. In the game of straws, we will always get the shortest one. Never forget that everything you do matters. The inability to monitor your alcohol intake indicates irresponsibility and shows a lack of control. Your image will be irreversibly tarnished.

The fear of being judged permeates every move I make. Over the years, I have observed how other minorities have been treated if they were deemed too radical, too boisterous, or too careless with their image. These missteps raised my antennae early on and they are still raised to this day.

I have a very extroverted personality and I love attending social events with libations. Connecting the dots about what could be said about me while taking into account my affinity for social settings and my love of cocktails, I decided early in my corporate career to limit my alcohol intake during work events. My sincere advice to you is to do the same. Limit your alcohol consumption during corporate functions to one or two cocktails, or glasses of wine, and space them far enough apart to minimize the effects.

If you are not a drinker, congratulations! You don't have to worry about mistakenly putting yourself in a compromising position. Non-drinkers only have to deal with the pressure of being coaxed into drinking because it's rare to find someone who doesn't drink. But for admirers of the grape, limiting alcohol consumption is mandatory.

Engaging in meaningful conversation about golf, politics, and family while taking a few sips at a company sponsored event is totally acceptable. By doing so, you're showing interest in what others have to say or what they do in their spare time. You are networking. These events are networking opportunities to further build internal relationships. Being an active participant in the moment shows that you're making an effort to fit into the environment around you.

Overindulgence is the enemy and I can guarantee that your behavior will be a whole chapter in the mental journal of the co-workers and leaders keeping track of your every move. You will not be given a pass. Your image has to remain unblemished as much as humanly possible. There are too many other aspects of the double standard to deal with, so do not create another unnecessary barrier. Be responsible. Be self-aware. Stay woke. Consequently, you can not "stay woke" if you are passed out on the floor. Protect your image. Know your limits.

The Calibration Discussion: We Talk About You!

Calibration discussions usually happen two or three times a year when it's time to evaluate individual job performance and promotion recommendations. Managers and executives meet to openly discuss whether job requirements are being met, highlight deficiencies, and share personal experiences that either support or defeat the evaluation.

Yes, I'm here to confirm that we talk about you. The good, the bad, and the ugly. All things are on the table to be discussed. The accolades are celebrated, but not without a counter perspective. Achievements are reviewed to call out exceptional levels of execution, then flipped to say there could have been more proactive updates to the leadership team. Please note that there is without a doubt some aspect of personal interpretations skewing every point of view.

Prior to the meeting, each leader is given a template, or questions, to answer about each person on their team. Feedback should be completed before the meeting occurs. Then, the documented notes pre- and post-meeting are consolidated and become a summary of your performance.

During a calibration, the next step of your career is determined in a matter of minutes. Managers make recommendations for promotions during this process. By the end of the meeting, all promotions have been discussed and the ones that get approved don't happen simply based on the manager's recommendation. All managers in the meeting have a voice that impacts the final decision. This discussion significantly proves that everything you do matters. The conversation resembles something like this:

Jane (Mary's manager)
"Mary has completed every assigned task with an exceptional level of execution. She's mentoring a couple of her peers who rely on her feedback, and really has proven that she understands the company goals and how her work supports those goals. Recently, when there was a server outage, Mary quickly stepped in to analyze the outage, pulling the performance logs leading up to the outage, which led her to the cause of the issue. Mary remained calm when there were several people reaching out to her for an update. Her communication was clear

and proactive. She's really done a great job over the past six months and she deserves to be promoted."

John (worked with Mary during the outage)

"I agree that Mary handled herself very well during the outage and remained professional at all times. However, I received feedback from my team that they were confused throughout the outage, and that while Mary communicated proactively to leadership, the project team did not understand what was going on. She seemed to be acting alone, and the team was frustrated with her lack of communication to them. I think she needs to work on her collaboration skills a bit more before she gets promoted. I'd like to see her take more of a leadership role in high-stress situations. Has anyone else seen this behavior from Mary?"

If similar feedback like John's is heard from other managers, Mary's promotion is put on hold just like that. The team and management involved in the incident were all watching and evaluating Mary's every move, and she probably didn't know she was being judged.

Executives are not exempt from calibration discussions either. There are seniority levels to the performance review. The managers evaluate individual contributors, directors evaluate the managers, the vice presidents evaluate the directors, the C-Suite evaluates the vice presidents, and the Board of Directors evaluates the performance of the C-level executives.

Accountability is required at every level. The discussions can be tough and often hard to hear, but the harsh reality is that the viewpoint, or perspective, of just one person can change the entire trajectory of your career. The hope is that executives always act with fairness at the helm, and that equality will prevail over biases that have the potential to skew the thoughts of the other leaders. For me personally in my executive leadership roles, I have a responsibility to call out blatant biases to ensure the criteria for each candidate being considered for a promotion is the same across the board.

The Politics of It All

Managing office politics is stressful, but it's a big part of understanding who ultimately has the final say in decisions that set the direction for the company. The political climate of a company is the blueprint to build your internal network and know how to leverage other people's influence in a way that benefits your personal career path. Therefore, managing office politics means you know that certain decisions are the culmination of input from multiple people (managers, directors, Vice Presidents, etc). The more potential a promotion decision may have to impact revenue, consumer experience, or employee satisfaction, the more involvement from other decision-makers you may think are outside of their purview or jurisdiction.

This is not to say that there is no freedom to make decisions at all, especially if you hold a leadership position. However, in certain situations you may not have the power to make the final decision.

The same holds true for career paths. Job performance has its place, but it's not the only thing you need to do to gain influence, leverage, and push your career forward. There's a strategy that accompanies job performance and career advancement. It's the politics of it all.

From my own experience, most people hate office politics and feel that it hinders progress. If you are among those who hold this belief, you are 100 percent accurate! Unfortunately, the consequence of refusing to employ a strategy to navigate your office culture may result in stagnation.

Complaining about office politics may also yield dividends of stagnation, and we're not interested in being stagnant. The concept of "shake the hand" and "kiss the baby" has been the biggest hurdle to overcome with my mentees. The screeching disgust in their voices as we talk about accepting office politics is undeniable. However, there's no way around it. Once you make the decision to seek executive-level positions, you have no choice but to mentally attach yourself to the need to schmooze—a little or a lot—depending on the company.

It's a chess game. The chess board is filled with key players in the game, and each one has a degree of power to move differently across the board based on their own status. Each move must be strategic. One wrong move will lead to an unwanted reaction and the overpowering and removal of multiple pieces from the game. Study the board so that you can predict the next two or three moves that could potentially follow. As Black women, we have to do more than our colleagues. Any benefit we can create for ourselves will help move us forward. Learn how to play and thrive at the game of office politics.

> **The Gift:** *Your persona as a leader is just as important as your leadership skills. Every move you make should intentionally place you in a strategic position. Present the best version of you at all times.*

> **The Perspective:** *Be attentive. Take the time to understand the dynamics of your organization and act accordingly. There will always be obstacles. Those obstacles are easier to deal with if you are mentally and emotionally prepared. Stay three moves ahead.*

10
They Tried It!

"Black women have to find their identity based on the culture of the company and figure out how to fit in."

Barack Obama was the forty-fourth President of the United States and the man who was hit with more double standards than can be counted. Small statements and gestures were blown completely out of proportion because he's Black. President Obama was met with constant opposition from Republican-controlled Congress during his second term, especially the final two years. They made it their business to block his proposals.

His citizenship was challenged because his father was Kenyan, while his predecessor was hardly ever criticized by his constituents. Off-the-cuff, over-exaggerated, incompetent behaviors and statements weren't as harshly scrutinized during the Bush administration. Yet every word from President Obama's mouth was dissected under a microscope and sometimes twisted to be offensive in an attempt to diminish his qualifications.

Living through the Obama era and witnessing blatant defiance of his leadership as President because of racism was shocking. It makes me angry to relive the challenges he faced only because of the color of his skin. President Obama suffered undo scrutiny, blatant disrespect, and bold-faced, uninhibited racism daily for eight years. Yet he still handled those daggers with unwavering poise, sophisticated style, and extreme resilience.

Meanwhile, many of his faithful supporters were at home screaming at the TV from their living room couches hoping that he would one day break character and give his Republican constituents a taste of their own medicine. He never did. Consequently, Obama's professional demeanor did not discourage attempts by his opponents to stir up drama. They tried every tactic possible to sabotage his position as the Leader of the Free World.

So when you hear the colloquial phrase "they tried it," you already know something shady and drama-filled has taken place. Urban Dictionary defines being "tried" as when someone steps to (approaches) you in a negative way to get a reaction from you and you do nothing in response to retaliate.

I've been tried many times. Too many times to count. I've been openly confronted with statements that were blatantly racist or sexist in nature, challenging my intelligence and/or my ability to perform in my role by men of all ethnicities, my peers, direct reports, and even other women.

Of course President Obama's list of challenges far exceeds anything I've experienced in my corporate career, but there are significant parallels in our respective journeys. And I honestly believe that if President Obama had been President Michelle Obama, her presidency would have been exponentially harder because of the compounding racial and gender biases that accompany being a Black woman. If she had run for President (like so many of us wanted her to), she would have stepped into the world of double standards AND double jeopardy.

Double Standards, Double Jeopardy

Let's face it—both attributes of being a woman and a minority come with long-standing, systemic, and institutionalized marginalization. The effects of being a double minority are deeply rooted. In fact, as Black women, we are held to a higher standard than our white male counterparts. My own eyes have witnessed these inequities. I have been subjected to these double standards, such as seeing certain privileges extended to my peers—affording them the flexibility and the immediate forgiveness of their actions—that were not extended to me.

All aspects of my personal performance as a leader have been heavily scrutinized. The hard reality is that gender and race heavily define experiences in corporate America. Remember, we have to work twice as hard just to be recognized as good enough. Black women have to find their identities based on the culture of the company and figure out how to fit in. Our work ethic and performance must exceed the baseline of others, and we must keep in mind that our mistakes are eternal when the mistakes of others are easily forgiven. Whether you like it or not, Black women are bound to high performance expectations with a low chance to recover from mistakes. Basically, Black women have to answer to a different level of accountability.

"We contribute to a current debate that focuses on whether individuals with more than one subordinate identity (i.e., Black women) experience more negative leader perceptions than do leaders with single-subordinate identities (i.e., Black men and White women). Results confirmed that Black women leaders suffered double jeopardy, and were evaluated more negatively than Black men and White women . . . these results suggest that Black women leaders may carry a burden of being disproportionately sanctioned for making mistakes on the job."[20]

The research has been done and there is one thing that is utterly clear–the consequence of being a woman and a minority is the perfect storm for racial and gender biases to negatively affect your corporate career. However, these God-given attributes are what make your view of the world unique. Companies are in desperate need of diverse thought leaders to support innovation who aren't afraid to challenge the status quo. Companies need you!

The research findings of how Black women have daily struggles in corporate America should be your fuel for motivation. The data shows difficulties but not one report says that it's impossible. Ursula Burns proved that. So, when you encounter double standards, dealing with the reality of what's happening should come naturally because you are mentally and emotionally prepared.

Mistakes are Not Allowed

At the beginning of my leadership career, I lost a lot of sleep and missed meals worrying about my job performance. Many nights I wondered what I did wrong as I tried to comprehend why I was treated differently.

The telecommunications industry is fast-paced. I knew that from my ten year tenure at one of the largest companies in that arena. I take pride in the work that I do. I hold my job

[20] Ashleigh Shelby Rosette and Robert W. Livingston, "Failure is not an Option for Black Women: Effects of Organizational Performance on Leaders with Single versus Dual-Subordinate Identities," *Journal of Experimental Social Psychology* Volume 48, Issue 5 (September 2012): 1162-1167.

performance and work ethic in high regard, and it's not due to arrogance or an inflated self-image. I genuinely want to do a great job using my talents to benefit my team, my organization, and my company. Nevertheless, the stress during my time there became unbearable and I started to question my own talents. I began to feel that my hard work, attention to detail, proactive communication, and efforts to team build and collaborate just were not enough.

I double-checked and triple-checked status updates and read my emails over and over to eliminate typos since I couldn't have any misspelled words in my emails. I met with my project teams and managers multiple times a week so I could stay connected to the latest update. But somehow, after meetings with the executive teams, I still felt inadequate. I began to notice that my questions were different, more in-depth regarding the most minute details. At that time it seemed like I needed to have a deeper understanding of the job and my role than my colleagues. I asked myself, "Do I need to do more?"

Everyone else around me didn't seem to have the same sense of urgency, and yet I seemed to be the one taking the brunt of the criticism. That one question, "Do I need to do more?" was one I did not have an immediate answer for and created an opportunity for me to internally hone in on what I perceived as my own incompetence. I felt like I had to be perfect ALL THE TIME! No mistakes allowed. I had to be Superwoman. But guess what? Perfection is impossible.

Not one person on this Earth is flawless. Not one. Not even Beyoncé. I've made mistakes and I've learned from each one. Mistakes are learning tools for growth. To unconsciously create self-doubt through unachievable expectations is unfair and unethical. The expectations we face as women, especially Black women, are higher than those others face. As we climb the ladder, the Black tax (the price for inhabiting spaces, roles, and positions where we are generally not found) we pay gets more expensive. The lesson here is to know that there will be times when your best is not good enough for others because of who you are. However, if you did your best, that's all that matters. You already know you are being seen through a different lens. Don't let other people's biases diminish your confidence level.

Blatant Disrespect is Not Okay

I have used my influence for positivity by calling out actions of racism, gender bias and disrespect. I know what it feels like to be treated unfairly and I'll never purposely do that to anyone. Being a catalyst to remake corporate America in a way that is more diverse and inclusive is my purpose and a calling I take very seriously. No matter who the person is, if I have the ability to positively influence a situation, I will. I've experienced a lot of different things in my career that were both shocking and disappointing, and I have done my best to turn those situations into teachable moments. I hope that bringing attention to issues of blatant disrespect, will help to create sensitivity, awareness, and respect for other cultures and ethnicities. Consider these examples:

Situation 1

I attended a meeting to review and finalize business requirements for a new project. My direct report was with me and held the title of Director. He was an Indian gentleman who joined the team earlier in the year. The purpose of the meeting was to gain an understanding of requested project changes for the new campaign system. As we began the document review, I saw a statement about an application feature that seemed contrary to the overview I read the night before. I asked that we follow up offline to validate the details.

With a raised voice, my direct report said, "I don't think that's necessary. I know this is right."

After a brief pause, I countered, "I'm sure this is accurate, but I still want to validate the details for our business partners. Let's move on."

He interjected, "No, Monica, it's right. No need to review."

At this point, it was going to get ugly, so I ended the meeting with a commitment to take more time to review the system documents. I ended the call, left the room with my direct report, and asked him to meet me in an empty conference room for a quick chat.

I explained to him that it's okay to disagree, but there is a way to do it. I told him that respect should always be given to others' opinions and that our relationship would not work without mutual respect. He agreed, apologized, and vowed to handle himself more professionally going forward.

But what made him think this was okay to do in the first place? My only conclusive answer to this question is that he perceived his privilege as being greater than the hierarchy of our positions within the company structure, or he was trying to save face so as not to look uninformed about the project. Whichever reason lived in his mind about why he felt the need or thought it was okay, to behave in the manner he did toward a superior was not okay for him, and will not be okay for you. Blatant disrespect, even if you don't perceive it as such, is intolerable.

Situation 2

I was on a conference call with a team of developers. The call included myself and two managers. I was the assigned project manager running the meeting. One of the developers began to provide an update on the progress made over the weekend. The developer was from another country and had a very heavy accent. The status update was less than favorable, which put the project delivery date at risk due to the lack of progress.

The manager's response was, "I can't do this with you people!"

I was offended and he wasn't even talking about me. I immediately apologized to the developer, ended the call, and proceeded to contact the manager's boss to report the offensive statement. The following day, I was met with an apology stating that his intent was not to offend. His level of awareness was low and needed to be addressed.

Situation 3

The weekly review meeting began and I was facilitating the call. More than thirty people joined the meeting either locally or remotely via a video app. During one of the status discussions, I was asked to provide an update on streamlining the acceptance review process for new work requests. I very thoroughly explained how the process was being defined, the amount of progress that had been made, and next steps. Or at least I thought I did. My boss at the time took it upon himself to re-explain what I said in an effort to bring more clarity.

My self-awareness got the best of me and I asked about five or six different people to give me candid feedback about my overview.

I asked, "Did you understand my overview? Was it vague or confusing?"

All of them assured me they understood exactly what I'd said, and went on to say that having my words restated in a different way did not add much value.

One person said, "I don't know why he did that!"

If my overview was clear to the meeting attendees then what drove the burning need to carbon copy and shuffle my explanation?

At this level, for my boss, it may have been the need to assert his authority. However, his actions were undermining my leadership and were read by my colleagues as unnecessary.

25

While he may have felt he was taking control, his statements came across as messy, invaluable, and to me, disrespectful.

Situation 4

I scheduled a 30-minute meeting with one of my peers to review the latest version of a business process change, explain the benefits of the change, and request the data I needed to complete the task. Since I had the overall responsibility to gather and analyze the data, getting buy-in and support from my peers was critical.

I made an extra effort to spend time with him and I answered all of his questions. The meeting ended with confirmation that he understood the impacts and supported the tasks planned for the upcoming weeks. The very next day, during our leadership staff meeting, I was asked to provide an update. Don't you know that the same person I spent a prolonged amount of time with explaining the project to looked right at my boss and said, "Can you explain the reason for this project? I don't understand why we're doing this."

WHAT IN THE HELL! *You can not be serious*, I thought. My mouth dropped open from shock. I was furious but had to keep my composure for the duration of the meeting.

Later that day, I sent him a text asking to coordinate a call and talk about our disconnect. He never responded. So, we spend all of this time together, I thought, I answered all of your questions, you leave our call proclaiming clarity and understanding, then you say something totally different in a room full of our peers.

From the outside, it looked like I had not done my due diligence. His lack of response to my request to talk about what happened during the meeting confirmed for me that he knew exactly what he was doing.

There is never a time when it will be okay to totally disregard another person. When you get into positions of influence, it is up to you to use that influence to make the workplace better. Fair treatment is mandatory for everyone. I know how it feels to be disregarded and feel invisible, and unimportant. How I treat people speaks volumes about my character. I will represent my team in the best way possible, showing respect even when respect is not given, and always advocate for equal treatment regardless of who you are or where you come from. Blatant disrespect is never okay.

Your Work Comes First , No Matter What

The second half of 2019 was the most difficult time of my life. My mother, who was living with me at the time, had major health issues resulting from manufactured drug injections. I am the primary caregiver for my family. By default, and rightfully so, I took the lead role during this family crisis. Days turned into weeks, and weeks turned into months.

No one in my family could have predicted such a long and difficult road to recovery for my mother. I soon realized I needed to make adjustments at work. I delegated some of my work to my management team and held on to a few key responsibilities. In hindsight, I should have delegated everything to my team, but I was afraid of being labeled a failure as if I couldn't balance the responsibilities of both home and work. I let my fear cloud my judgement, and as a result, I made mistakes.

Mistake 1

I was given the option to take a week or so off from work or continue to be a part of the team. Not understanding what was happening to my mother, I chose to stay on and try to do it all.

Mistake 2

My focus should have been on my family first. I made my job more important than the care of my mother.

Mistake 3

I trusted my leadership to understand what I was going through and allow flexibility in my hours. Instead, I faced more intense scrutiny when I expected empathy to prevail.

My leadership turned on me and failed to support me during my most vulnerable time. Everything I did was emphasized ten-fold, whether good or bad. For example, there was an incident where I put together a slide for my boss to discuss during a town hall meeting. When the time came to review my slide, I selected a different version of the slide—same details, different look. Once the screen came up, I quickly made the adjustment to the more familiar version. My boss was visibly irritated. I immediately sent a text to apologize for the mix-up and offered to set up a time with him to discuss what happened. I got no response.

A few days later, I got an email citing concerns with my recent performance. I reached out to our administrative assistant asking for a 30-minute meeting. She scheduled the time. I also scheduled time to meet with my HR Lead. During the call, no one asked about the status of my mother's condition. There were only matter-of-fact statements related to his expectations going forward. I graciously accepted the feedback and ended the call. Next up was my meeting with HR. By the time the meeting started, I could not hold back my tears. This was the one time in my 20-plus year career where I let my vulnerability show and I didn't care.

The pressure became unbearable. To know that the only thing on my boss' mind was a slide when my mother was literally in the hospital fighting for her life was beyond upsetting. His lack of empathy infuriated me to the core, but I shouldn't have expected anything different. All I kept thinking was that I should have taken the time off, but the fear of being labeled as inadequate led me to choose otherwise. The unknown of how long it would take for my mother to recover also played a big part. I didn't know what I didn't know. From that time on, I felt my time at my job was constrained. My focus was off. I could not believe my Superwoman powers were failing. I was unable to balance requirements between home and work. I felt like I had failed!

Consequently, my mother's condition only got worse as the weeks went by. Instead of feeling the unwavering support from my direct leadership, I felt scrutinized. The empathy for me was nonexistent. I guess you could say that since I made the choice to stay, I had to be accountable for my performance. Maybe you're right. But deep down, I believe that if the situation had been reversed and one of my subordinates had been juggling responsibilities at work and at home, I never, ever would have lost sight of the human side of leadership. Regardless of my decision to stay active at work out of my own fear of failure, I believe my superiors should have been more empathetic and understanding. Yes, I made mistakes, and I paid for them over and over again.

Similarly, one of my direct reports experienced their own personal turmoil during this time. Her mother was extremely ill and not expected to live through the coming weeks. When my team member got the call, she was on a plane the next day to India. While traveling, she took the time to send me and her direct manager a very detailed message and a plan of how she would work while she was in India with her family. My answer to her was, "We got this. Please take care of yourself and your family. We will figure out how to support your work until you return."

They Tried It!

Within days of her arrival, her mother passed away. Bereavement is not the time to create anxiety over a job or give an employee something else to worry about. Family ALWAYS comes first. But the one thing I have seen with my own eyes is that empathy gets lost when leaders are unable to see the value in extending an understanding hand to employees.

Now, let's get back to my situation, in which I was not afforded the same concern. As a matter of fact, the more my mother's condition worsened, the more difficult conversations with my boss became. Were there a few misses? Yes! Did I ensure all areas were covered when I realized that I needed to focus more on my mother? Yes! I met with my leadership team to let them know that I needed their support during this time. Each one of them agreed to support me without hesitation. I was also very transparent with my boss about what was going on. Yet even with that level of transparency, there was still a high level of expectation for me to continue to perform in the midst of a significant family emergency.

My mother's condition began to stabilize as the months proceeded but there was a long way to go before she reached total recovery. Daily visits to the hospital were still required. Coordinating drop-off and pick-up for her afternoon appointments was stressful, but it had to be done. I did my best to support and balance my responsibilities at work and at home. I showed up every day at work with the intention of erasing the sins of the recent past, overcompensating and overextending myself to revive what I felt was a dying work relationship. Was I paranoid? Was I putting undue pressure on myself to be perfect ALL THE TIME? Maybe. But deep down in the core of my belly, I can't help but believe that more leniency would have been granted if I looked different.

In this circumstance, it was evident that assumptions and preconceived notions about my strength as a Black woman—that I brought onto myself as I tried to do it all—were used against me. In this moment when I needed compassion and empathy, I was met with more exacting demands, discontent,

111 Monica M. Brown

and displeasure when I stumbled. As I said before, mistakes are not allowed, even the ones that are unintentional. I was put into a position where I had to prioritize between work and family. I chose my family, but oftentimes as Black women climbing the corporate ladder, we're expected to choose work.

The Gift: *Balancing a thriving career and family is challenging. Forgive yourself for the mistakes. It's okay to lay down your cape sometimes. Your best IS good enough!*

The Perspective: *Never let anyone make you doubt your greatness. If one company doesn't appreciate you, go to another one.*

11
The Next Level

"Our perspective is needed to force a higher level of respect for diverse points of view."

At this point, you have either made it to the C-Suite or you've taken the time to focus on laying a solid foundation to get there. There's a clear understanding of the inner workings of who you are and how your presence alters the behavior of those around in your professional network. This is great. A strategic plan is in place and the blueprint is set. The next level is within reach and doesn't seem so far away.

While aspects of the path forward may still seem exaggerated, unnecessary, and fake, you can rest assured knowing that you have the essential steps to propel your career forward. However, putting those steps in motion is the key to the next promotion, and the next promotion, and so on. Persona and relationships will get you there. Confidence, resilience, and ambition will keep you there. Your experiences are valuable. Your ability to lead is powerful.

I've talked about the inevitable obstacles ahead to equip you with enough knowledge to gracefully handle potential scenarios. You now have the ability to recognize what's happening to you while you are in the moment, then consciously react accordingly, instead of realizing what transpired after the fact, which is what has always happened to me. Your foundation is solid, firm, and strong, and your dream is attainable. You must realize that our perspective as Black women is needed to force a higher level of respect for the diverse points of view which drive companies to achieve success. We are more than capable of leading any organization. Now that we're moving up to the next level, everyone within physical and virtual reach must know it, too.

We Are Magical and Everyone Needs to Know It

A key factor in becoming a catalyst for change is to bring awareness to the masses as often as possible and to emphasize the urgent need to diversify corporate leadership. I'm a firm believer that knowledge is power. My voice is powerful. Your voice is powerful. Our experiences are real because we are real human beings. Every effort to silence our voices as Black women or women of color to diminish our views should serve as your daily motivation. The more we speak on the impurities of corporate oppression, the more opportunities we create for ourselves to exist and take up space while also destroying unwarranted perceptions of Black women.

Should you choose to walk this path of vocally expressing to the world the need to eliminate gender and racial biases, make sure you speak from the depths of your heart and soul. Bring others into the emotions you felt when you've fallen victim to overt and passive racism. Once you've reached a level of professional success, it's easy to become comfortable in your career. It is important, however, to actively seek out ways to keep the conversation–about your struggles, failures, and triumphs to get where you are–going, never losing sight of the benefits of open dialogue about general and personally specific obstructions.

In the age of social media, there are multiple free platforms available to spread the word and advocate for change with access to millions of people who may share your point of view. You can utilize digital platforms to inspire other women of color who aspire to be Vice Presidents and Chief Officers. With only a few faces that look like us, a chance to showcase an achievement is validation to other women to say they can do it, too. Inspiring posts, encouraging videos, pictures, networking events, speaking engagements, panel discussions, and career day at local schools are all outlets to talk about your experiences and your career. Your accolades are like badges of honor. Wear them proudly.

LinkedIn is the top professional social networking site in the world. It's the perfect place to increase your professional visibility and promote your recent career achievements. Take the time to make your profile stand out by providing vivid job descriptions from past and current employers. Use the platform to demonstrate your ability to accomplish company objectives as well as personal goals.

Your accomplishments certify that you've mastered the skill sets necessary to be an effective leader. An attractive LinkedIn profile coupled with sharing an undeniable passion for leadership and upward career progression could open the door for a new position. Personally, I've secured two leadership roles through LinkedIn. For the first job I secured through LinkedIn, I posted about my interest for an open position, received a call from the Human Resources Coordinator a few days later, completed twelve rounds of interviews, and was presented with a job offer a few months later. For the second job I secured through LinkedIn, a recruiter contacted me after viewing my profile and following my posts for months. There's nothing wrong with creating visibility of your career achievements for strategic advantages. It increases the chance of getting noticed by hiring managers seeking diverse talent.

Another way to expand your reach is to volunteer for organizations where you can become a mentor to young girls and other women seeking career advancement advice. Volunteering is a great way to give back. You'll feel a sense of pride knowing you gave your time and talent to worthy people. The gratification of knowing that someone's life has changed simply based on the encouragement you've given them in a short period of time makes all the bumps and bruises you experience navigating your career and climbing the corporate ladder worthwhile. Feeling a sense of purpose is beyond explanation.

Non-profit organizations, schools, and training groups are excellent mediums to share personal career stories, leave a positive impression, and possibly impact the world for generations to come. The tools you impart to others—like this book you're holding now—are solid building blocks to be used to boost their own journeys. Seeing yourself standing in front them makes the dream real. Attainable. Achievable. Possible! You've worked hard. WE'VE (collectively) worked hard. Don't be afraid to show it. Share the details of your journey. Encourage young girls and women of color that it can be done.

I Can See the C-Suite

I'm optimistic that change in the face of the corporate structure is coming soon. I'm extremely hopeful that the percentage of Black women in Vice President and C-Suite positions will increase to 10 percent by 2030. Right now, we currently represent less than 1 percent of Fortune 1000 top-level decision-makers.

The seemingly upward trend of hiring women of color is worth celebrating, but we have a long way to go. I've made it my personal responsibility to positively influence my surroundings by plowing through miles of steep grass and tall trees to remove as many roadblocks as possible. Since the onset of my first director role in 2012, I've been committed to mentoring anyone determined to propel themselves into a leadership career. I even began to work with my own executive coaches while interacting with some of the top level executives in the country. I have accepted every request to be a panelist to discuss various topics from my own personal experience and career path. I also speak at events and use these opportunities and platforms to show my face as a force to be reckoned with—not in an arrogant way, but to say, "Yes, I'm here to represent for the other women of color on their way up to the top."

Achieving a goal that's seemingly impossible to obtain is what motivates me to continue moving forward. It's what I've deemed the pinnacle of my career. I'm always asking, "What's the next level?" Once I achieve that goal, I ask the question again, "What's the next level now?" It's a never-ending loop for me until I'm able to hold the title I've set as my goal. I continue to be fueled by my ambition and pushed forward by my motivation.

The next goal for me is making it to the C-Suite. Breaking the glass ceiling is mandatory and I have my sledgehammer ready to swing. As you now know, it is rare to see women of color—especially Black women—achieve such an accomplishment and own such a title. Even the slightest increase to the "less than 1 percent" representation is worthy of extreme fanfare. It deserves exaggerated celebration. WHEN I've reached the goal of C-level executive, I plan to share the details of my passage into the unknown with you, continuing my mission to leave a trail of breadcrumbs for others to follow.

I'm still learning and I am always open to enhancing my leadership prowess. No leader is above keeping their skills sharp and up-to-date. For me, it is a must. Leadership conferences, technology summits, training classes, and online research are all ways to stay abreast of market trends and maintain a competitive edge. Essentially, we've talked about the top skills to support ascending to the top. Relationship-building, the ability to communicate effectively, strategic innovation, and empathy are core competencies of the top CEOs in corporate America. I have laid the foundation of knowledge, skills, emotional intelligence, self-awareness, resilience, and empathy. The culmination of all those characteristics is the perfect recipe for a *bad ass* leader. All I gotta do is make it to the top!

> **The Gift:** *Make the vision plain - decide what you want to do with your career and do it! Create strategic alignments along the way while mapping out the steps to get there. Be confident. Be bold. Be intentional.*

> **The Perspective:** *Remember that diamonds are created under pressure, those bumps and bruises will serve as proof of your ability to endure and persevere. The next level is right at your fingertips.*

12
The Room Scan

"I plan to do as much as humanly possible to serve as a catalyst to influence the pipeline of diverse talent going up to the top."

A few times during the year, select companies will schedule strategic planning meetings or some variation of a small conference away from the office. The multi-day sessions are usually held at a hotel or event center capable of accommodating large groups. Only the top-tier leaders are invited to attend these closed planning sessions. At the company's expense, folks travel from different locations to convene for the purpose of setting the short-term and long-term goals for the upcoming year(s). The first day is loosely scheduled to allow out-of-town travelers to arrive and get settled. Soon enough, the hotel bar will become the gathering spot to greet the other attendees. After a few drinks (only two for you), everyone retires to their respective rooms, getting some much-needed rest to mentally prepare for the next day's planning activities.

I've attended my fair share of these meetings. There's nothing like the feeling of getting dressed up in business attire and walking into a room of roughly twenty-five to more than one hundred executives—depending upon the size of the company and the number of leaders invited to attend. The number of people in the room becomes a moot point once you realize that you are either the only Black leader in the room, or sometimes one of two, maybe three if I'm being a little ambitious with the count. I know this because the first thing I do when I walk to such rooms is "the room scan." I pan the room with my eyes as I silently ask myself, *How many of us are in here?*

Any person of color who has spent time in a corporate environment has done this at least once. I've scanned many a room in a matter of seconds. Why? The reality is, I'm likely going to be the *only* Black person in attendance, and definitely the *only* Black woman.

If by circumstance more than one of us is in the building, we connect via eye contact for a long stare and a gentle "what's up" nod. Then I begin to run across the room slowly with my eyes as if it were a scene in a movie. I'm always happy to see a familiar face. As I approach the other Black person in the room, I always wonder, *Is this real? Could it be true?* I introduce myself to strike up a conversation, and I start by asking and learning more about their role, location, and responsibilities. Then suddenly, I can hear Michael Jackson's "You Are Not Alone" playing in the background. (Kidding.) But if a theme song was ever needed for this situation, that would be the song.

Assessing the surroundings of the room helps the assessor (in this case me, or you) connect with how much *representation* is needed to get through the meetings. It's akin to being on the inside of a boxing ring, bouncing up and down, waiting for the bell to ring.

Round 1

It's time to step into the ring as the astute leader you are to prove that you are here to stay. Gaps in representation gives you time to mentally prepare to represent and get in the right mindset. In these rooms, every second you're there, you represent—not only yourself, but others just like you who may not be as far up in the ranks—and continuously prove that not only do you belong, but you deserve to be there.

Round 2

I know deep down that I'm not the only person who does this. Others may not admit to this silent ritual of scanning a room and counting the people of color within it, but I'm willing to bet a few pennies that this method of surveillance happens very, very often. And although I'm specifically sharing accounts from my corporate experience, I'm extremely confident this behavior spans all industries from media and entertainment to fashion, retail, etc. When we do this—the room scan—you know, like I know, that we are looking for a familiar face to ease the tension of being alone, of being the only one.

To take it even further, I start calculating the percentage ratio in my head. The number is usually 2 or 3 percent minority representation. Calculating the number of Black women averages less than 1 percent. This truth hurts. There should be more people of color, women of color, especially Black women, at these meetings holding high-level leadership positions.

It's not that there are no qualified Black women available. This is the lie corporate America (and many other industries) tries to perpetuate, but it is false. There are plenty. Factually, we are not sought after during the recruiting process. The focus for diverse recruiting typically comes as a mandate from Human Resources, or the Diversity and Inclusion team after they've reviewed the deficit of diverse talent within the company.

Don't get me wrong—any help we can get to launch the executive careers of more people of color is accepted and appreciated. I don't view targeted recruiting as a handout. Every crack in the door is an opportunity, regardless of the initial intention behind it. It's an opportunity to break down a wall and clear the way so that the person coming behind you can walk in more easily.

Round 3

The room scan is the rawest way to describe what happens during the first 30 seconds of entering a room. Each time a room scan is done, it validates what is already known—Black women are underrepresented and this lack of representation motivates those invested in influencing and changing the status quo to keep going. It's the ugly truth that slaps us in the face. It's a reality requiring efforts to diversify corporate America to be constant and persistent. I stand firmly on the belief that change is inevitable, but only if there is a continued march toward the goal of diversifying and appreciating a different point of view, thus creating true inclusivity.

One of these days, there won't be a need for me to search for other minority women as if I'm participating in a treasure hunt hoping to find the ultimate prize. One of these days, I'm going to attend a leadership meeting, company town hall meeting, or travel to a strategic planning meeting somewhere in the world alongside other top-tier leaders and immediately feel proud. I won't need to scan, count, multiply, or divide to confirm that the lack of diverse talent is still an issue. And even if the charge extends beyond my God-given years, I plan to do as much as humanly possible to serve as a catalyst to influence the pipeline of diverse talent going up to the top.

Reach Back and Pull Forward

As I continue to grow in my career, I have to share the lessons I've learned with anyone who will listen. Although the context of this book is to increase the pipeline of Black women leaders at the executive level and beyond, we can not do it alone. A supporter, influencer, or sponsor could be anyone willing to fight for equal opportunities and equal pay for underrepresented women of color. We are human beings first who must be judged by our character, leadership acumen, and experience, not by skin color or where we were born or who we choose to love.

In my experience, allies who advocate for gender and racial diversity genuinely want to help alter the way people think and change the institutionalized practices hindering the progression of Black women and other marginalized groups. Their advocacy is necessary, and in most instances, their voices will resonate, forcing the shift from prejudice to progressive thoughts and actions. The benefits of alliances like these are invaluable to pulling us forward.

My story is just one piece of the puzzle. As I pour into aspiring Black women executives, my hope is that the seeds planted—here and elsewhere—will shape the budding careers of the next generation of Black women executives. That woman—whoever she may be—will then pour into another minority woman to shape her career, continuing to pay it forward.

I use the leverage I've gained to reach back and pull someone else forward. One way I do this is by tapping into my network to solicit candidates for open jobs on my team or within my organization. Referring qualified, diverse candidates for consideration is a great way to present otherwise overlooked talent. Basically, it is our job to lift as we climb. My eyes may be looking at what lies ahead, but my arms are extended, and my hands are open and ready to tightly clutch the hand of another to pull her up with me. It's how we guarantee that our presence at the table is never questioned and never becomes extinct.

Corporate America Needs You!

Whew! I know it seems like a lot to comprehend: knowing what to say, how to act, mastering skills, communicating effectively, being a thought leader, being empathetic, finding a mentor, and if you're lucky, gaining a sponsor. Not to mention that these attributes come in addition to the management of your racial and gender identity: don't be too black too soon, but be proud of who you are, display emotional intelligence (don't be "The Angry Black Woman"), assimilate with the culture, but don't lose yourself in the shuffle . . . the list of requirements is long and not for the faint of heart. There will be days when it's mentally and emotionally heavy. I've been there many times.

I remember driving to work one morning in tears, sobbing because my personal life was in shambles. I was a mess as I moaned the entire trip. By the time I turned into the building driveway, my tears were gone and I walked into the office ready to work. I had to suck in all of my emotions to have a productive day. The show must go on.

On another occasion, my leadership skills were openly challenged by an employee who made it seem that their sole purpose in life was to see me fail. It didn't matter what I did to show support and concern, the relationship continued to be strained, and then it escalated to Human Resources. I was frustrated that I was unable to fix the situation, but I knew I had done the right thing and needed to move on. I took comfort knowing I did my best to do right by my employee and turned it into a lesson learned.

Another hard, emotional lesson I learned, was one my mother tried to teach me early on. I recall staying up all night working on a presentation to show the roadmap for the thirteen lines of business I owned and the status for every single project in those respective areas. The stress was unbearable. I was already in a situation where I felt like everything I did was heavily scrutinized. I was under a microscope and could not make any mistakes. I spent days pulling data together for senior leadership consumption. The night before the meeting, I was up all night reviewing what I had compiled. By this time, I had put so much pressure on myself it physically manifested as severe stomach pains. I managed to do what my mother told me not to do, and that's "worry myself sick."

I've sacrificed a cumulative amount of months away from home in the name of my corporate career. So much so that I came home one day and my youngest daughter was taller than me. I struggled to remember key moments I spent with her throughout the year. I was on the road so much, that I actually woke up and could not remember what city I was in. I realized my family time was gone and I would never be able to get it back. It's all a part of the sacrifice, but eventually I had to learn the word "balance."

Finding Work-Life Balance

The push and pull of work-life balance is a very sensitive and challenging topic, especially for women. The work-versus-home scenario can oftentimes turn into a dilemma, and you will eventually have to deal with the sensitivities and impacts of the never-ending dynamic.

The struggle of work-life balance tends to impact women more than men because of the role we play within the family. As women, we have multiple, daily, critical responsibilities at home within our families in addition to our job responsibilities. Things like making breakfast and dinner, packing lunch, getting the kids off to school, helping with homework, driving to soccer practice, and attending the school play where your son or daughter has the leading role. It's the push and pull of competing priorities that is difficult to manage. My hope is that for women who have a significant other, the daily tasks of home are split in such a way that both parents have assigned duties. This way one person doesn't have to do it all alone. For other women who, like me, are single parents, we *have* to do it all—or in the very least, figure out the best way to do as much as we can.

The amount of time and attention required to maintain the responsibilities of both home and work is astronomical. There aren't enough hours in the day to do everything we feel we need to do. One side will eventually suffer if priorities are not managed with robotic precision. I have yet to meet someone able to perfectly execute work-life balance. And no, splitting your body in half or cloning your DNA is not an option. There will always be ebbs and flows. The key is how you manage when both sides are ebbing and flowing in demand of your attention at the same exact time. The obvious answer should be that family comes first. However, the scales will hardly ever be equally divided, and in the moment, it is not always easy to decipher or decide which *priority* truly comes first.

When my career began to thrive, my family suffered. When my family needed my time and attention most, it required me to minimize time toward my office duties. Feelings of guilt and inner turmoil are real, and I didn't want to fail. Black women want to do it all and we want to be good at everything. Well, truthfully, it's not that we want to do it all, but oftentimes we just don't have a choice. I felt so guilty during both situations. I was unaware of how to create harmony in my life. The stress became unbearable. For me, my work-life balance was working in the office all day and working from home all night. Obviously, this model of spending most of my time working was not sustainable. Work-life balance is something I still have to work on consciously, consistently, and constantly.

Over the years, I decided to implement a few tactical steps to hold myself accountable and carve out more time for my family.

1. **Forgiveness:** I had to learn to forgive myself. I am my worst critic. So putting pressure on myself to do everything all the time AND make no mistakes was unrealistic. I have turned those experiences into life lessons.

2. **Create Boundaries:** Define your family expectations. They all want to see you and you want to love on them. Put boundaries in place, like no laptop at the kitchen table or only critical work calls

on the weekend. The time you'll gain turns into valuable time to spend with your loved ones.

3. **Speak Up:** Communicate those boundaries to your boss and peers. Explain your family commitments and work directly on a plan for support. Ensure that your boss understands how important family is to you. Proactive communication builds trust amongst the team and shows integrity.

Jobs come and go. As one door closes, others will open. If I'm ever made to choose between my job and my family, there's no debating that my family will always and forever come first. And for those of us who aren't afraid to go hard for a long time, remember that mentality is the exact opposite of one that drives both personal and career-changing decisions and rarely ever leads to the balance we need to be healthy and whole in both of these important areas in our lives.

Final Thoughts

Your success becomes the success of every Black woman. The fight is bigger than just you! It's bigger than just me. What we achieve within our careers allows other Black women to excel in ways we have yet to imagine. The biases can only be torn down by one awkward scenario we encounter at a time. In this way our experiences and the struggles we've overcome lower the hurdles and remove the obstacles intended to hold us—and those coming up behind us—back. Our struggle is our reality. It's a shared burden and we have to bear to eliminate the normal practice that is discrimination. Because we are twice as likely to be overlooked due to intersectionality, it is imperative to use our voices to demand fair and equal treatment at work.

My path has taken me from dropping fries at Mickey D's to an administrative assistant in the media industry to the title of

Vice President. If you gain nothing else from this book, please know that you can achieve whatever goal you set for yourself if you are willing to do what is necessary to make it happen. Learn the rules of the game. It's the *only* way you will ever win. Then, WHEN you achieve the status of being a *Bad Ass* boss in corporate America because you have successfully and literally fought your way to the top, the collection of everything you had to go through to achieve the goal of reaching the executive level will give you a sense of pride and accomplishment that can never be taken away from you. You did it. You earned it. Wear it like a badge of honor, embrace the unicorn you are, and let your black girl magic flourish. Sis, you are the shit!

The Gift: *Once you have achieved a position of influence, you become a gift to others. Use it wisely. Share the blueprint to executive excellence by giving explicit details on what to do, how to do it and how bias-based incidents made you feel.*

The Perspective: *A solid plan for career advancement is mandatory. Strategic moves must be put in place to yield results. If things don't go as expected, make another plan. Your career requires constant evaluation. As events happen, do what is required to adjust and keep going. You are not allowed to give up - ever!*

Perspectives
Views from Black Executives in
Corporate America

Julie M. Wenah
Airbnb Community and Africa Regional Counsel
Founder, The Album and The Mixtape

My whole life has been rooted in working overtime. When I was sixteen years old, my friend from church created a website—back when the dot com industry had just taken shape—and she nicknamed all of her friends in the site. Some were named "The Intellect" or "The Athlete." You want to know what I was named? Drumroll please . . . wait for it . . . "The Workaholic." The craziest part is I didn't take offense. I wore it like a badge of honor.

I am a child of immigrants. I watched my father being deported out of my family home at seven years old. At that moment, at just seven years, old I made it my mission to always provide for my family. Since I've gotten older, I've gone to therapy and done the shadow work to face those parts of myself that needed confronting and healing. But at sixteen, being deemed "The Workaholic" was alright with me.

My workaholic nature has led me to work for some of the best organizations doing important work for mankind, such as with NASA, and the Obama Administration, and many other incredible opportunities that could only be the result of the prayers of my ancestors hailing from the rural parts of Nigeria.

As women of color, we are often taught at an early age to work hard. We're taught that working hard will get us light years ahead when that couldn't be furthest from the truth. Solely working hard is not the answer to advance your career. The goal is to do excellent work that brings tremendous value to your organization's mission and, bottom line, with minimal confusion. This means regulating your emotions when people not only tap dance on your last nerve, but bust a split after they did a triple pirouette on that same nerve.

Remain nimble to pivot, but remember your North Star. Your North Star is your home. It is your guiding light. It is the calling that you have over your life.

Even though these corporate and organizational systems aren't intuitively created to advance and grow women of color, staying rooted to the calling you have over your life can help you grow your career path and excel, no matter the institutionalized obstacles before you.

Nikki M. Baker
Vice President, Program Management
Marriott Bonvoy

As I sit and reflect on my career, I think about what has shaped me into the person that I am today. There are many varying factors from the inspiring words of people whom I have connected with, to the lessons that I have learned from failures over the past twenty-plus years. With that, I have had great experiences that have given me the tools to pursue opportunities to advance my technology career to executive leadership with an industry-leading company.

My story as an African American woman in corporate America in technology is unique, but there is certainly a common perspective that is shared between myself and other women of color no matter the industry.

Each time that I have accepted a new leadership position, I am always hopeful that there will be other African-American women working with me who are my peers or are in higher positions with whom I can identify and learn more about the different challenges and paths to success specific to our journey. More often than not, I am disappointed.

It's even more disheartening when attending extended leadership meetings for all executives in technology. Of the meetings that I have attended, there are always less than five African-Americans in any given room during the entire conference. This includes men and women. Each time I'm face to face in these scenarios, I go through a range of emotions.

Early in my career, seeing a lack of African-Americans around me as I began to advance in my career confused me. And what began as confusion ended only in frustration. Over the years, as I've come to understand that this scenario of lack of representation, diversity, and inclusivity is unfortunately the norm, I have quickly realized that I must be part of the solution. I must be a catalyst for change.

It's become my personal mission to ensure that I do my part in creating opportunities for other African-American women, be they in my immediate organization or across the wider company. My emotions now start and end with excitement. The fewer African-American women I see in the rooms I enter for my industry, the more inspired I am to change the dynamic.

Art Hopkins
Russell Reynolds Associates

For far too long, many girls got their first taste of navigating a career with babysitting. When their male counterparts were being instilled with the principals of "driving a hard bargain" and "getting what you're worth," girls were taught to ask for "whatever you think is fair."

Far too many of these young women have begun their careers with this ideological ballast weighing them down. As they begin to assert themselves in their careers to gain altitude, they must avoid the ever-present danger of crossing the invisible line of being assertive versus being aggressive. For their male counterparts, the latter is often a reputational badge of honor. For men in corporate environments, being labeled as "aggressive" is synonymous with being "demanding," "tenacious," and "having high expectations." For women in the same exact environments, the "aggressive" label is often the kiss of death.

For Black women, the challenge is compounded by the threat of your assertiveness and your aspirations. You could easily earn the label of "the angry black woman" whether you're deserving of it or not. Furthermore, not only are there far too few Black women to serve as mentors, sounding boards, and advocates for others or within a company structure. Often if there is a Black woman in that role, she is likely the *Only One*.

Monica Brown's book sheds light on these realities and provides all of us with the invaluable perspective of one of the few who has traversed this gauntlet through corporate America and risen through the ranks to the executive level.

Notes from the Next Generation

Mom,

You are the hardest working woman that I know. I am extremely proud of you and all that you have accomplished and will continue to accomplish. Everything that you set your mind to you do. You achieved your goals without letting anything or anybody get in the way. If I had to choose one word that described you it would without a doubt be resilient. You have beaten all the odds that have come your way, and I could not ask for a better role model. My prayer is that this book touches the lives of many. May you continue to inspire those who may feel that all the odds are stacked against them and that they have no way to accomplish their goals and dreams. You are my personal Superwoman. Thank you for being an amazing mother!

Love You,

Keva B.

To my Mom,

I am so honored to call Ms. Monica Brown my mother. She has come so far in her career. She inspires my every single day. I want to be just like her when I grow up. She is a strong, independent, intelligent, caring, determined, outgoing, confident, creative, responsible, charismatic, humble and hardworking leader. Growing up, she always made sure I had everything I needed and more. She makes me laugh and smile every single day. Her ambition level is through the roof. I know there's nothing she can't achieve or conquer. I am so proud of my mom.

Your daughter,

Madison

Acknowledgements

My Grandmother, Albertha (Berta) P. Williams, your hard work and sacrifice was not in vain. I thank you for being the perfect example of unconditional love. You were a pillar of strength for our family and, to this day, I feel you in heart and soul. You are my forever true love.

My mother, Gloria, is the strongest person on this earth! A true definition of a fighter. God chose the perfect angel to nurture me into the woman I am today. I love you and thank you for showing me what it looks like to never give up!

My father, Louis, is the hardest working man in South Carolina. He taught me the value of working hard and told me to always focus on my goals. There was never a doubt in my mind about his love and unwavering support. Thank you so much, B-Daddy. I love you!

To my children, Keva and Madison, know that I love you beyond time and existence. You are both so talented, majestic, and perfect. Thank you for tolerating my silliness, stubbornness, and my absence when I had to leave you to go to school and work. Please forgive my imperfections. You are my foundation and the reason I decided to never stop striving for excellence.

To my best friend since middle school, Auntie Robin, you are what the words "selfless" and "sacrifice" look like. You will give the clothes off of your back without hesitation, never once considering your needs. We've shared gut-twisting laughter and heart-wrenching tears. We are joined at the hip! God knew what he was doing when he put us together. He knew that you needed me just as much as I needed you. Love you, Honey! Forever.

To the first boss to see leadership qualities in me, Lewis Simons, although I didn't understand what you were doing at the time, your influence is still relevant in my career today. Thank you for seeing something in me that I didn't see in myself.

To my colleague and friend, Trenton Parks, your referral led to my first leadership role which proved the importance of having a strong network. All it took was one phone call. I didn't know I was ready until you reached out to me. Thank you!

To my mentor and friend, Michael "Doc" McCrimmon, it's an honor to know you and to call you my friend. Thank you for your candid points of view along with your mentorship over the years. Having your stamp of approval is priceless because I know you don't give that away often–if at all. I don't take your support for granted and I cherish our unbreakable connection. Thank you!

To my current boss, Justin Reilly, I've only known you for a short period of time, but I want to thank you for being the leader I aspire to be. The fact that you genuinely care about people and celebrate diversity is a welcomed breath of fresh air. You are the perfect example of how a top-level leader can be human, too!

To everyone I've talked to about my career challenges and triumphs, I can still hear every word of encouragement you've given me. Thank you.

Bibliography

1. "About: What is Diversity & Inclusion." *Global Diversity Practice*. https://globaldiversitypractice.com/what-is-diversity-inclusion/.

2. Hunt, Vivian, Sara Prince, Lareina Yee. "Delivering through Diversity." *McKinsey & Company*. January 2018. https://www.mckinsey.com/business-functions/organization/our-insights/delivering-through-diversity.

3. Larson, Erik. "New Research: Diversity + Inclusion =Better Decision Making at Work." *Forbes*. 21 September 2017. https://www.forbes.com/sites/eriklarson/2017/09/21/new-research-diversity-inclusion-better-decision-making-at-work/#77835e84cbfa.

4. Eurich, Tasha. "What Self-Awareness Really Is (and How to Cultivate It)." *Harvard Business Review*. 4 January 2018. https://hbr.org/2018/01/what-self-awareness-really-is-and-how-to-cultivate-it.

5. Forsey, Caroline. "The True Meaning of Self-Awareness (& How to Tell If You're Actually Self-Award)." *HubSpot*. 11 May 2018. https://blog.hubspot.com/marketing/self-awareness.

6. Simonvil, Pierre E. "Code Switching: Does it Help or Hurt Diversity?." *New Jersey State Bar Association*. February 2019, https://community.njsba.com/blogs/njsba-staff/2019/02/22/code-switching-does-it-help-or-hurt-diversity?ssopc=1.

7. "Code-Switching." *Oxford University Press*. 2019. https:// www.lexico.com/en/definition/code-switching.

8. Dosh, Kristi. "Golfers Make Better Business Executives." *Forbes*. 16 May 2016. https://www.forbes.com/sites/ kristidosh/2016/05/16/golfers-make-better-business-executives/#69176bd7b4a5.

9. "Key Data Highlights on Equity and Opportunity Gaps in our Nation's Public Schools." *U.S. Department of Education Office for Civil Rights*. 7 June 2016. https:// www2.ed.gov/about/offices/list/ocr/docs/2013-14-first-look.pdf.

10. "About: Our Mission." *Information Technology Management Forum*. 2017. https://itsmfonline.org/ about-itsmf/.

11. Stobierski, Tim. "How to Become a More Empathetic Leader." *Northeastern University*. 2 August 2018. https://www.northeastern.edu/graduate/blog/become-an-empathetic-leader/.

12. Paese, Matthew Ph.D., Evan Sinar, Ph.D., Audrey Smith, Ph.D., Bruce Watt, Ph.D., Rich Wellins, Ph.D. "What's the Number 1 Leadership Skill for Overall Success?." *Developmental Dimensions International*. 23 February 2016. https://www.ddiworld.com/global-offices/ united-states/press-room/what-is-the-1-leadership-skill-for-overall-success.

13. Stych, Anne. "HR Professionals are Overwhelmingly White Women." *The Business Journals*. 27 February 2019. https://www.bizjournals.com/bizwomen/news/latest-news/2019/02/hr-professionals-are-overwhelmingly-white-women.html.

14. Stych, Anne. "Percentage of Women in C-Suite Roles Inching Up." *The Business Journals*. 24 April 2019. https://www.bizjournals.com/bizwomen/news/latest-news/2019/04/percentage-of-women-in-c-suite-roles-inching-up.html?page=all.

15. Smith, Alexis Nicole, Marla Baskerville Watkins, Jamie J. Ladge, Pamela Carlton. "Interviews with 59 Black Female Executives Explore Intersectional Invisibility and Strategies to Overcome It." *Harvard Business Review*. 10 May 2018. https://hbr.org/2018/05/interviews-with-59-black-female-executives-explore-intersectional-invisibility-and-strategies-to-overcome-it.

16. "Your Guide to Salary History Laws by State and Locality," *Salary*. 2020. https://www.salary.com/resources/guides/salary-history-inquiry-bans/.

17. Rosette, Ashleigh Shelby and Robert W. Lingston. "Failure is Not an Option for Black Women: Effects of Organizational Performance on Leaders with Single Versus Dual-Subordinate Identities." *Journal of Experimental Social Psychology*. Volume 48, Issue 5 (September 2012). 1162 - 1167.

18. Joint Economic Committee United States Congress. "Gender Pay Inequality: Consequences for Women, Families and the Economy." *A Report by the Joint Economic Committee Democratic Staff*. April 2016. https://www.jec.senate.gov/public/_cache/files/0779dc2f-4a4e-4386-b847-9ae919735acc/gender-pay-inequality---us-congress-joint-economic-committee.pdf

About the Author

Monica M. Brown is a deeply-accomplished and results-driven senior executive. She has worked for several Fortune 500 companies, including AT&T, Comcast NBCUniversal, and SiriusXM Pandora. Monica has received multiple awards for her contributions to the IT industry. In 2016, she received the Women of Color STEM Special Recognition Award and was featured in the 2017 and 2018 Edition of *Who's Who in Black Atlanta*.

Monica has also served as a mentor for multiple organizations, including the Information Technology Senior Management Forum (ITSMF). Monica holds a B.A. in Professional English and Broadcast Journalism from South Carolina State University and an MBA from the Michael J. Coles School of Business at Kennesaw State University.

She has two daughters, Keva and Madison, and currently lives in Atlanta, Georgia. Her hobbies are golfing, shopping, traveling, and writing. *Only One* is her first book.

CPSIA information can be obtained
at www.ICGtesting.com
Printed in the USA
LVHW031030220720
661208LV00003B/188